THE STEP BY STEP ART OF
Making Soft Toys

THE STEP BY STEP ART OF
Making Soft Toys

Text and Soft Toy Designs by
ALAN DART

CHARTWELL
BOOKS, INC.

Published by
CHARTWELL BOOKS, INC.
A Division of **BOOK SALES, INC.**
110 Enterprise Avenue
Secaucus, New Jersey 07094

CLB 3321
© 1994 CLB Publishing Ltd, Godalming, Surrey
Printed and bound in Singapore by Tien Wah Press
All rights reserved
ISBN 0-7858-0075-1

AUTHOR'S DEDICATION

For Peggy Gray,
who first encouraged me to pursue a career in
design, with much love.

ACKNOWLEDGEMENT

The publishers would like to thank
Staks Trading Ltd, 31 Thames Street,
Kingston-upon Thames, for supplying
properties for photography

Managing Editor: Jo Finnis
Editor: Adèle Hayward
Design: Nigel Duffield
Photography: Steve Tanner
Photographic Direction: Nigel Duffield
Illustrations: Geoff Denney Associates
Typesetting: Mary Wray
Production: Ruth Arthur; Sally Connolly;
Neil Randles; Karen Staff; Jonathan Tickner
Director of Production: Gerald Hughes

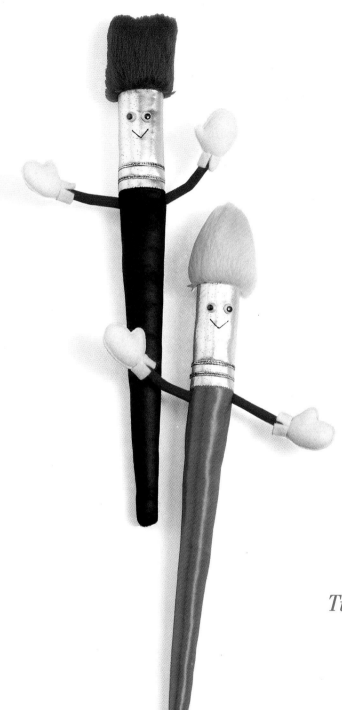

Contents

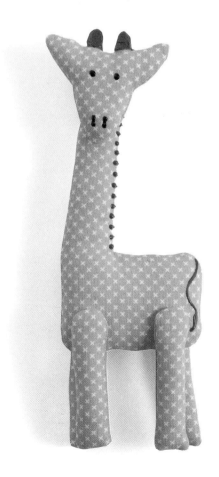

Equipment

For Cutting Out

You will need a pair of sharp **dressmaker's scissors** *for cutting fabric and a pair of sharp, pointed* **embroidery scissors** *for smaller pieces and for trimming, notching, and clipping seams.*

Keep another pair of scissors solely for cutting out the pattern pieces. Card and paper will dull the cutting edges and will make these scissors unsuitable for cutting out fabric successfully.

A **sixway hole punch**, *or a* **wad punch** *with a selection of cutters, is useful if you need to cut out tiny circles of felt for eyes.*

For Marking Out

To draw out or trace off the pattern pieces you will need a sharp **HB pencil**.

To mark out the pattern pieces on fabric use **tailor's chalk** *or a* **dressmaker's chalk pencil**. *Dressmaker's pencils are especially useful when marking out small pattern pieces. Neither will mark the fabric permanently, and can be removed by rubbing or brushing gently.*

Embroiderer's marking felt-tipped pens *can also be used to mark out light-coloured fabrics. Marks will disappear within 24 hours, while those made with a water-soluble pen need to be painted with clean water using a fine paintbrush to make them disappear.*

For Sticking and Sealing

With all glues, first check on a scrap of fabric to make sure that they don't seep through to the right side or affect the fabric's colour.

Use a general-purpose **clear adhesive** *to seal the back of felt and to glue small fabric pieces.*

Rubber solution glue *is used when you need to glue large surfaces together, or want an immediate bond on smaller pieces. Spread the adhesive on both surfaces. Once both layers have become touch dry, press together firmly. This type of glue does not allow for repositioning.*

A **hot glue gun** *is very useful when you need to attach glue-on joggle eyes, or need a secure and rigid join on larger pieces. Once applied, you have only 15 seconds to position the pieces before the bond is made.*

Spray adhesive *makes an even, low-tack, surface which is an especially useful way to hold difficult fabrics together for appliqué. It is also used when gluing charted, or photocopied, patterns on to card to make longer lasting templates. When spraying with the glue, it is most important to protect the surrounding area with plenty of newspaper, to work in a well-ventilated room,*

and to avoid inhaling the vapour. You should also look for a brand which is CFC free.

Anti-fray fabric sealer *is drawn round the cut edges of fabric and, once set, the edge will be sealed and need not be hemmed, or oversewn, to prevent fraying.*

For Sewing

Ensure that sewing machine needles are correct for the fabric you are working on. When sewing jersey fabrics it is important to use a **ball-ended machine needle**. *Standard machine needles cause laddering.*

You will also need long **dressmaker's steel pins**, together with **handsewing needles** for finishing off. To work the features you will need a selection of long needles – look for packets marked either 'long darners' or 'soft sculpture'.

For the Patterns

Dressmaker's graph paper is divided into 5 cm (2 in) squares. This is used when enlarging the charted patterns within this book to full size. Calculate 12.5 cm (5 in) squares on this paper where required.

Use **tracing paper** to trace off the same-size patterns and transfer them to paper or card.

Use **card** to make more durable and long-lasting patterns It is stout, but thin enough to fold in half and cut out double when required.

Some of the patterns are given in the form of measurements only. To draw up these pattern pieces you will need a **ruler**, a **set square** and a **pair of compasses**. A **plastic circle template** is useful when drawing out small circular pattern pieces.

For Positioning

A pair of round-ended long-handled **tweezers** is most useful to hold small pieces such as toy eyes and felt dots when spreading with glue and positioning on the toy.

Materials

Fabrics

You may substitute fabric specified in the materials' lists with others of your choice. However, it is most important that you replace a woven fabric with another of a similar weight. Always use a knitted fabric in place of jersey as these toys have been designed to allow for stretch.

Stuffing

The following stuffing materials can be substituted for one another when making many of the projects in this book, although PVC granules are really only suitable for the smaller items.

For general stuffing use a **washable, synthetic toy filling**. This is bulky yet light and will give an even finish to your toy. Do not try to economize by using a cheaper, inferior quality filling made from fibre waste. These always give a lumpy, ungainly appearance to the toy, as well as making the toy heavy and unwieldy.

Foam chippings can be used instead of toy filling to make a bath or swimming pool toy. The toy can then be wrung out and hung up to dry.

Polystyrene beads are used to make lightweight beanbag toys. Fill the toy only about three-quarters full with the beads as this will allow for movement..

PVC granules, or **dried split peas** and **lentils**, are fillings for small beanbags which can then be used for juggling or playing 'catch'. Do not use dried pulses in beanbags which might get wet.

Terylene wadding is used to pad pieces which need to remain flat and is available in thin, medium and heavy weights.

Interfacing

Non-woven iron-on interfacing is used to back fabrics which are thin or fray easily. **Very fine interfacing** will alter the thickness of fabric only minimally and is useful when marking on and sewing up tiny pieces.

Iron-on quilting interfacing is slightly padded, has diagonal quilting lines printed in white and is backed with adhesive. Only the quilting lines adhere when ironed on. Sew over them by machine, working from the back of the fabric.

Iron-on bonding web is used for appliqué. It is fused to the wrong side of the fabric with an iron, then the pattern shape is drawn on to the web's silicone backing paper. You can then cut round the shape, peel off the paper, position where desired and fuse in place. This web is also useful for bonding two pieces of fabric wrong sides together to make a non-fraying material which can be cut out and used without sealing the cut edges.

Threads

Use **standard sewing thread** for all the projects. Use a matching shade of **buttonhole twist** when sewing by hand as this is stronger than normal thread, can be pulled up tightly without the fear of it breaking and makes a more secure join. The features are embroidered with a variety of **cotton embroidery threads** as well as **cotton knitting yarns**.

Craft Components and Haberdashery

Toy eyes, wooden and **plastic beads, wood plaques** and **wheels, ribbons, fabric paints, Velcro** and **zips** are all readily available from department and craft and haberdashery stores.

Techniques

Cutting the Patterns

The patterns throughout this book appear in one of three styles - same size, charted, or measurements only. See pp. 12–13 for making the pattern pieces.

Mark all grain lines, arrowheads and dots on to the pattern pieces. The arrowheads are used to match pieces together. Cut out a small 'V' shape in the side of the pattern piece to allow you to mark the fabric at that point. You may also wish to make a tiny snip in the fabric at these points when cutting out. The dots are used either to match up with an arrowhead or to mark the position of the eyes. The grain line should always run parallel to the fabric's selvedge. This is especially important on jersey fabrics where there is more stretch across the fabric than there is parallel to the selvedge. If you are using a fabric with a nap, have the nap running upwards on each pattern piece.

The amount of fabric quoted for each toy is generous. However, you should lay out the pattern pieces on to the fabric first to make sure you can fit them in easily. Always mark out the pattern pieces on to the wrong side of the fabric, pinning paper pattern pieces in place, or holding card pattern pieces down with a paperweight while marking.

To Enlarge a Pattern

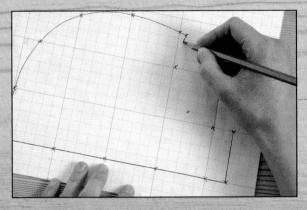

To enlarge a pattern use 5 cm (2 in) squared dressmaker's graph paper and follow the pattern to make a cross on the graph paper wherever the pattern outline crosses the lines. Join up these crosses with a pencil line to draw out the pattern shape. If you need to add a seam allowance, do so at this stage, then cut out the pattern piece.

Cutting a Pattern Piece on the Fold

If you are instructed to place a broken line on the fold do this when drawing out the pattern. Either:
1 *Chart the pattern piece on to a folded sheet of graph paper, placing the broken line on the fold of the paper.*

2 *Trace off the same size pattern piece and transfer to a folded piece of paper or card, again placing the broken line on the fold. Cut out the pattern piece from the folded paper or card and open out flat before marking on to the fabric.*

Making a Card Pattern

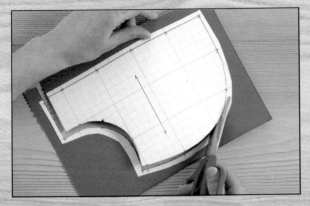

Marking Out a Pair

Card patterns are much more durable and long-lasting than paper ones and it is advisable to cut these patterns if you intend to make the toy more than once. Either transfer the same-size patterns directly on to card using tracing paper, or roughly cut round the charted or photocopied pattern pieces, glue to card with spray adhesive and cut out.

Measurement-only patterns are drawn directly onto the card following the measurements given.

1 When you are instructed to 'cut one pair' of a particular pattern piece, do not cut out the pieces from folded fabric but mark out each piece separately. First draw round the pattern piece with chalk, having the top side uppermost, then remove from the fabric.

2 Now turn the pattern piece over to the reverse side, place on the fabric and draw round with chalk as before. Repeat the procedure if you need to cut more pairs of this pattern piece.

Eyes and Noses

Although certain types of eyes are stipulated for each project, the final choice must remain at the toymaker's discretion, as they will know whether the toy is being made for a baby, toddler, older child or adult. Glue-on eyes and beads are not suitable for toys which will be given to babies or toddlers and should be substituted with either embroidered or sealed felt versions. The following selection of eyes can be used on most of the projects in this book so experiment and create your own special characters.

Toy Eyes

Glue-on: *Hold the toy eye with a pair of tweezers and cover the back with either clear adhesive or glue from a hot glue gun. Position with the tweezers, then press and hold in place for a few moments with your fingers until the glue has set.*

1 Safety eyes: *These instructions also apply to safety toy noses. Spread a little clear adhesive round the marked eye position on the wrong side of the fabric and leave to set. Now cut out, or punch, a hole which is large enough for the shaft of the eye to fit through.*

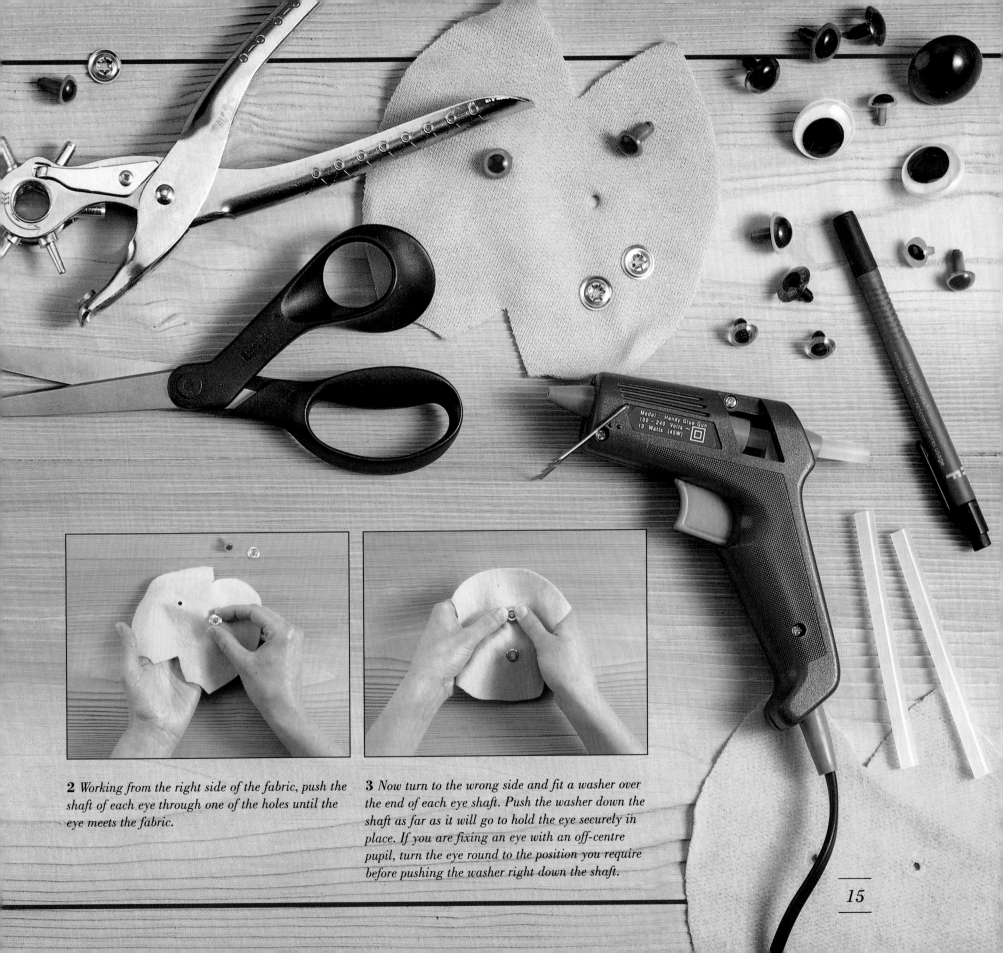

2 *Working from the right side of the fabric, push the shaft of each eye through one of the holes until the eye meets the fabric.*

3 *Now turn to the wrong side and fit a washer over the end of each eye shaft. Push the washer down the shaft as far as it will go to hold the eye securely in place. If you are fixing an eye with an off-centre pupil, turn the eye round to the position you require before pushing the washer right down the shaft.*

Fabric Balls

1 *Cut a circle of fabric and work a running stitch with buttonhole thread close to the outside edge.*

2 *Draw up slightly to make a cupped shape, then fill with toy stuffing and draw up further, filling with more stuffing if required to make a firm ball.*

3 *Draw up the thread completely to close, then fasten off securely with a French knot and trim off the excess thread. A woven fabric circle will make a round ball, and a jersey circle an oval ball.*

Sealed Felt

  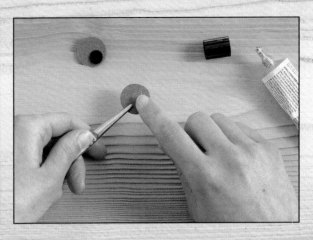

As felt is a non-woven fabric, made from compressed fibres, small pieces easily disintegrate. You can stop this happening by sealing the felt.

1 Spread some clear adhesive over the back of a piece of felt and rub gently into the fabric with your fingertip, making sure that the glue does not seep through and mark the right side. Leave the adhesive to set until hard.

2 Mark out the pattern pieces on to the sealed side of the felt with a chalk pencil and cut out. You can cut small circles with a sixway hole punch.

3 Glue the felt pieces together using a pair of tweezers to hold the pieces as you spread glue on the sealed side, then glue in place on the toy, using the tweezers to position.

Sewing and Finishing Seams

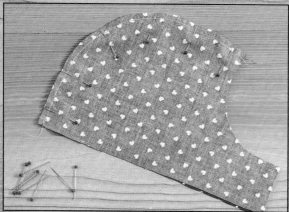

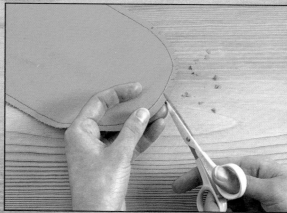

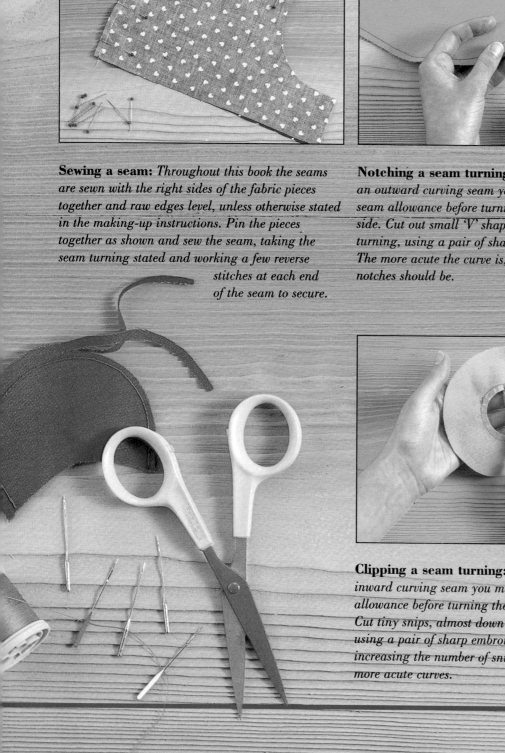

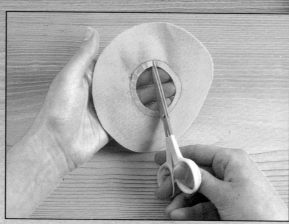

Sewing a seam: *Throughout this book the seams are sewn with the right sides of the fabric pieces together and raw edges level, unless otherwise stated in the making-up instructions. Pin the pieces together as shown and sew the seam, taking the seam turning stated and working a few reverse stitches at each end of the seam to secure.*

Notching a seam turning: *After you have sewn an outward curving seam you will need to notch the seam allowance before turning the piece to the right side. Cut out small 'V' shapes within the seam turning, using a pair of sharp embroidery scissors. The more acute the curve is, the closer together the notches should be.*

Clipping a seam turning: *After you have sewn an inward curving seam you must clip the seam allowance before turning the piece to the right side. Cut tiny snips, almost down to the sewing line, using a pair of sharp embroidery scissors, increasing the number of snips on the more acute curves.*

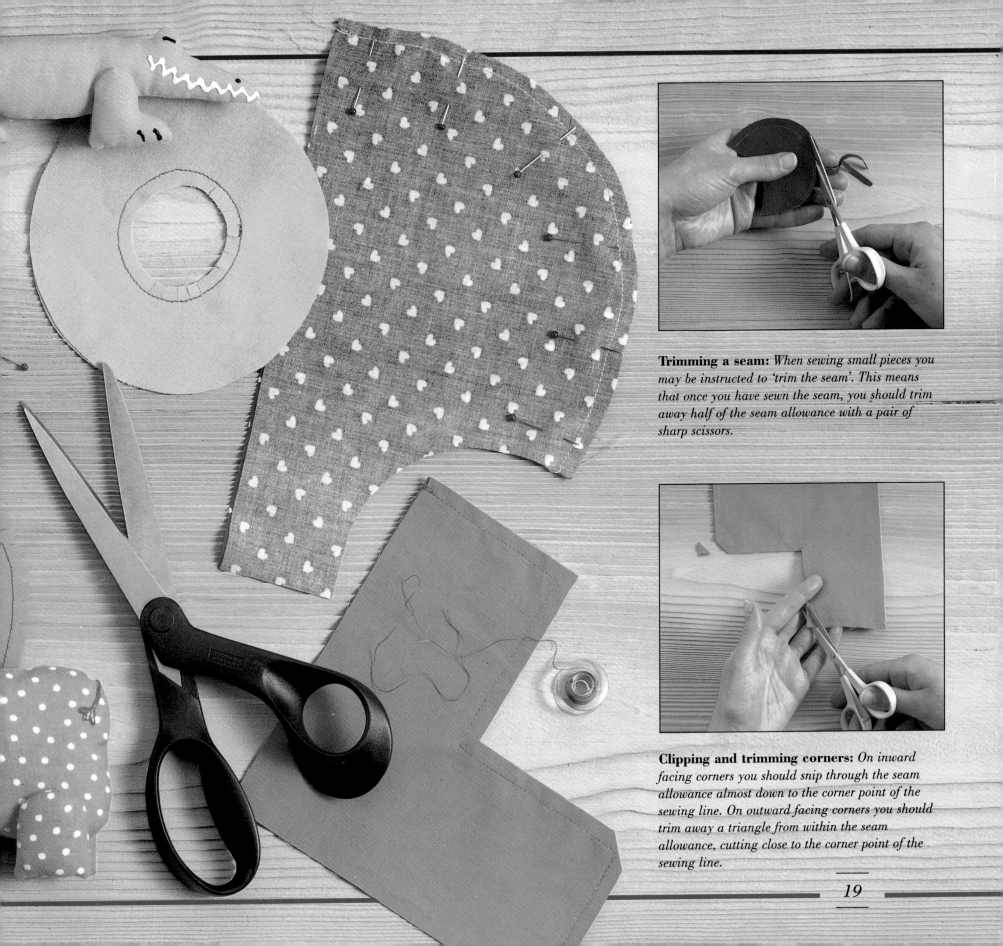

Trimming a seam: *When sewing small pieces you may be instructed to 'trim the seam'. This means that once you have sewn the seam, you should trim away half of the seam allowance with a pair of sharp scissors.*

Clipping and trimming corners: *On inward facing corners you should snip through the seam allowance almost down to the corner point of the sewing line. On outward facing corners you should trim away a triangle from within the seam allowance, cutting close to the corner point of the sewing line.*

19

Ladder Stitch

Gathering

Ladder stitch is used to handsew across an opening in a seam once the toy has been stuffed, and also to sew on fabric ball eyes and noses. Where an opening occurs it is advisable to work a line of machine stitching the same measurement as the seam allowance in from each raw edge before stuffing the toy as this prevents the opening from stretching and also provides you with guide lines for handsewing the opening closed. For extra strength, use buttonhole thread and take one stitch from one side of the opening, then take an equal-sized stitch from the other side, sewing just outside the machine stitched lines. Repeat several times, then draw up the thread to bring the two sides together. Work in this manner to the end of the opening, then fasten off securely and trim away the excess thread.

Gathering by hand: *This is used when you need to pull up the gathers tightly, condensing a lot of fabric into a small space. Use buttonhole thread for extra strength and work a row of even running stitches along the piece to be gathered, sewing close to the edge. Draw up the thread as directed in the instructions and fasten off securely.*

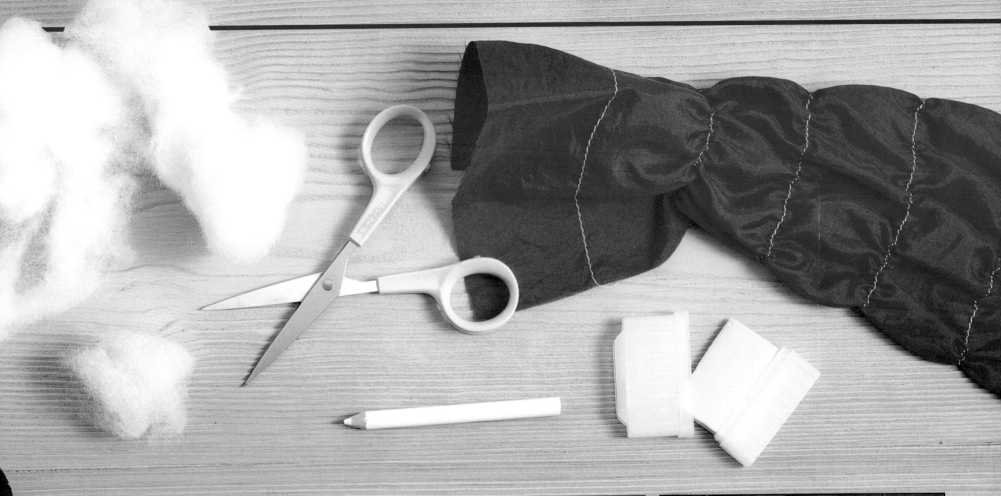

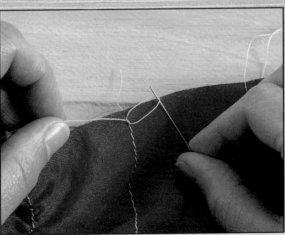

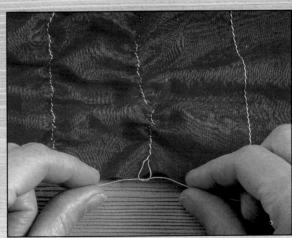

1 Gathering by machine: *This is used to make small, even gathers and to draw up a piece of fabric to a required measurement. Set the stitch length on your machine to its longest and loosen the top tension slightly. Work the lines to be gathered, leaving lengths of thread at both ends of each line.*

2 *Using a pin, draw the under thread up to the top of the work at each end of the stitched gathering line, then knot both threads together at one end.*

3 *At the opposite end, gently pull the under thread to gather the stitching up to the measurement you need, then tie the top and under threads together as before, trim off the ends of the thread and arrange the gathers evenly.*

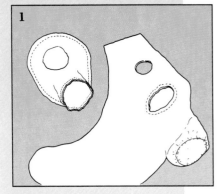

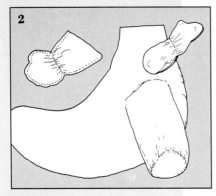

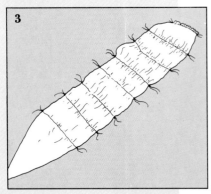

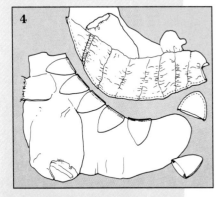

STEGOSAURUS

1 *As the fabric is quite slippery, you will find it easier to tack the pieces together before sewing rather than use pins. Sew the outer and inner leg pieces together, leaving the base edges open. Work a gathering thread round the base edge (see p. 20) and draw it up to fit the sole, tie off the ends of the thread, then sew the soles to the legs. Turn the legs to the right side through the hole opening then, with right sides together, sew legs to body pieces, matching arrowheads.*

2 *Work a gathering thread along the wrist line on each arm piece (see p. 21), draw it up to measure 7 cm (2³/4 in) and tie off the ends. Sew the contrasting arm pieces together, leaving the straight top edges open. Clip the turnings (see p. 12) at the base of the thumb, then turn the arms through to the right side. Sew into the opening on each body piece, matching the arrowheads on the body with the arm seams.*

3 *Work a gathering thread 6 mm (¹/4 in) in from each end of the short sides of the front gusset piece. Work a further six gathering threads across the gusset at 5 cm (2 in) intervals. Draw up one end thread to measure 7 cm (2³/4 in) and tie off the ends. This will become the neck edge. Draw up each of the remaining threads to measure 11 cm (4¹/2 in), tie off the ends, then sew the tail edge of the gusset to the curved edge of the tail gusset piece.*

4 *Sew one side of the front gusset and tail gusset piece to one body piece, matching the arrowheads on the body with the gusset seam and with the dot at the end of the tail gusset. Take two fin pieces right sides together and sandwich them between two pieces of*

You Will Need:
40 cm (¹/2 yd) of 150 cm (60 in)
wide red shell suit nylon
20 cm (¹/4 yd) of 150 cm (60 in)
wide orange shell suit nylon
10 cm (¹/8 yd) of 150 cm (60 in)
wide green shell suit nylon
A scrap of cerise shell suit nylon
10 cm (¹/8 yd) of 150 cm (60 in)
wide fine Terylene wadding
A pair of 24 mm (1 in) diameter
safety toy eyes
A scrap of iron-on interfacing
250 g (9¹/2 oz) of toy stuffing
Matching sewing threads

Cutting Out:
Enlarge the charted patterns on pp. 24, 26–27 to 200% (either on a photocopier or on to graph paper –see p. 12). Cut the front gusset, tail gusset, soles, and one pair of arms from orange, the mouth pieces from cerise and the fin pieces from green. Also cut a set of fin pieces from wadding. Cut all the remaining pieces from red.

Take 6 mm (¹/4 in) seam turnings throughout.

wadding. Sew all round, leaving the base edges open, then turn to right side. Make up all eight fins in this manner. Starting 15 mm (⁵/8 in) down from the neck edge, and spacing 6 mm (¹/4 in) apart, sew five of the fins to the back edge of the remaining body piece.

5 *Sew the opposite side of the gusset to the remaining body piece, then sew both body pieces together along the back seam, leaving the neck edge and the space marked at the base of the tail open. When joining the body back seam, follow the previous sewing line of the fins. Work a row of stitching 6 mm (¹/₄ in) in from each cut edge of the tail opening to prevent the fabric fraying and stretching.*

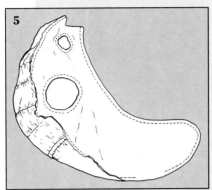

6 *Starting 15 mm (⁵/₈ in) up from the neck edge, and spacing 6 mm (¹/₄ in) apart, sew the remaining three fins to one head piece. Work a gathering thread round the front edge of the upper and under jaw pieces, draw each up to fit the mouth pieces, tie off the ends, then sew the jaw pieces to the mouth pieces.*

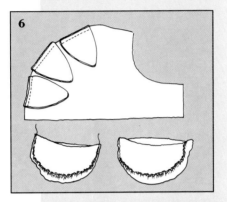

7 *Sew the head pieces together along the top edge, following the fin stitching line as on the body. Work a gathering thread round the front opening of the head between the arrowheads and draw up to fit the base edge of the upper jaw, then tie off the ends. Sew the base edges of the mouth together, then sew the upper jaw to the gathered head opening, matching the ends of the mouth seam with the arrowheads on the head and the arrowhead on the upper jaw with the top head seam.*

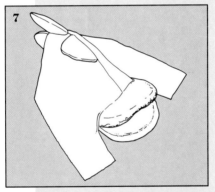

8 *Join the head front seam, then sew the under jaw to the remainder of the head opening, matching the arrowhead on the under jaw with the front head seam. Turn the head to the right side, work a gathering thread round the neck edge, draw it up to measure 21 cm (8¹/₂ in) and tie off ends.*

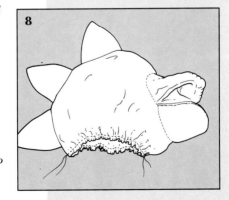

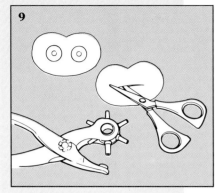

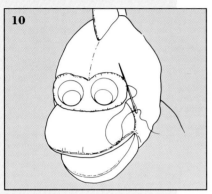

9 *Fit the head into the neck opening of the body and sew together, matching the back seam of the body with the top seam of the head and placing the front seam of the head in the centre of the neck edge of the front gusset. Turn through to the right side and stuff lightly so that body remains soft and slightly flexible, then ladder stitch across the opening (see p. 20). Cut two 2 cm (³/4 in) diameter circles of interfacing and fuse them to the wrong side of one eye mask piece directly behind the eye positions. Punch, or cut, holes at eye positions to fit the shafts of the toy eyes. Cut a slit opening on the other eye mask piece, cutting between the two eye positions.*

10 *Sew the eye mask pieces together all round the outside edge, then turn it to the right side through the slit opening. Fix the eyes in place (see pp. 14–15), then stuff the mask firmly and oversew the edges of the opening together. Position and sew securely to the head with ladder stitch.*

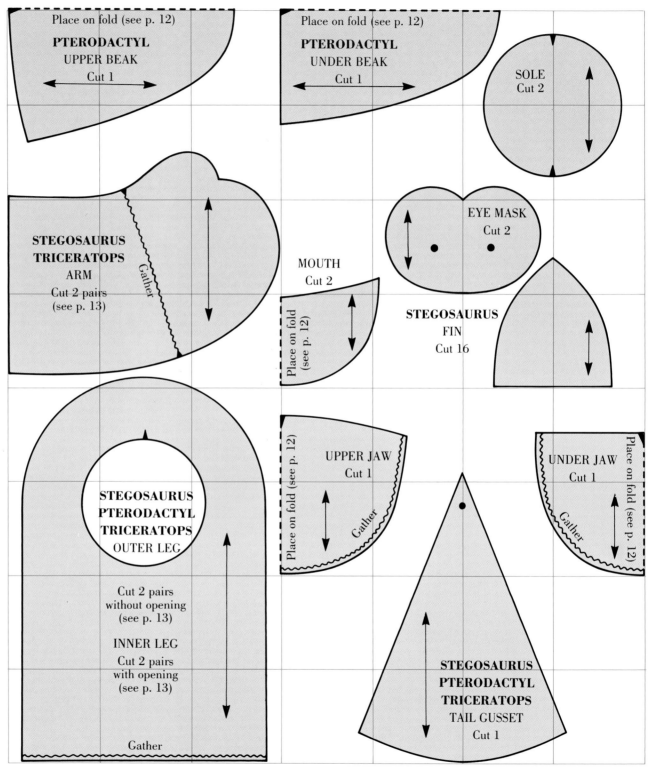

DAFT DINOSAURS CHARTED PATTERNS: 1 sq = 5 cm (2 in)

Daft Dinosaurs

TYRANNOSAURUS CAP

You Will Need:
A cotton drill baseball cap
20 cm (¼ yd) of 115 cm (45 in)
wide blue cotton chintz
A small amount of blue and
white spotted cotton fabric
A scrap of red cotton chintz
40 cm (½ yd) of white
ricrac braid
A pair of 24 mm (1 in) diameter
safety joggle eyes
A scrap of iron-on interfacing
75 g (3 oz) of toy stuffing
Matching sewing threads

Cutting Out:
*Enlarge the charted patterns on
pp. 24, 26–27 to 200% (either
using a photocopier or by
charting on to graph paper – see
p. 12). Cut out one pair of arms,
an upper and under jaw, eye
mask pieces and a head from
blue chintz, adding 2.5 cm (1 in)
to the base edge of the head
pieces. Also cut one pair of arms
from spotted cotton and the
mouth pieces from red chintz.*

*Take 6 mm (¼ in) seam turnings
throughout.*

◀ *Adults and children alike
will love such unusual,
three-dimensional headgear
with its brightly-coloured
contrasting cap. Be prepared
to attract a lot of attention
– and to be asked to make
more than one!*

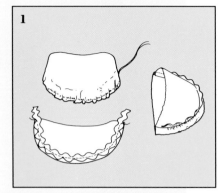

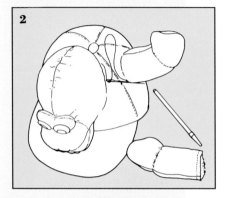

1 *Sew ricrac round the outer edge of the right side of both mouth pieces. Gather the upper and under jaw pieces and sew to the mouth pieces as for the stegosaurus (step 6) following the previous braid stitching lines. Make up and stuff the head as for the stegosaurus (steps 7–8), drawing up the gathers tightly. Make up the eyes as for the stegosaurus (steps 9–10).*

2 *Make up the arms as for the stegosaurus (step 2), working a line of stitching 6 mm (1/4 in) from each open top edge before stuffing. Pin the head in place on the front of the cap. Inside the cap, draw a 7 cm (2³/4 in) diameter circle with a vanishing marker pen behind the dinosaur head. Sew the head in place with backstitch, using the marked circle as a guide. On the outside of the cap ladder stitch (see p. 20) the arms to two 5 cm (2 in) diameter circles at the arm positions, sewing along the stitched lines at the top edges.*

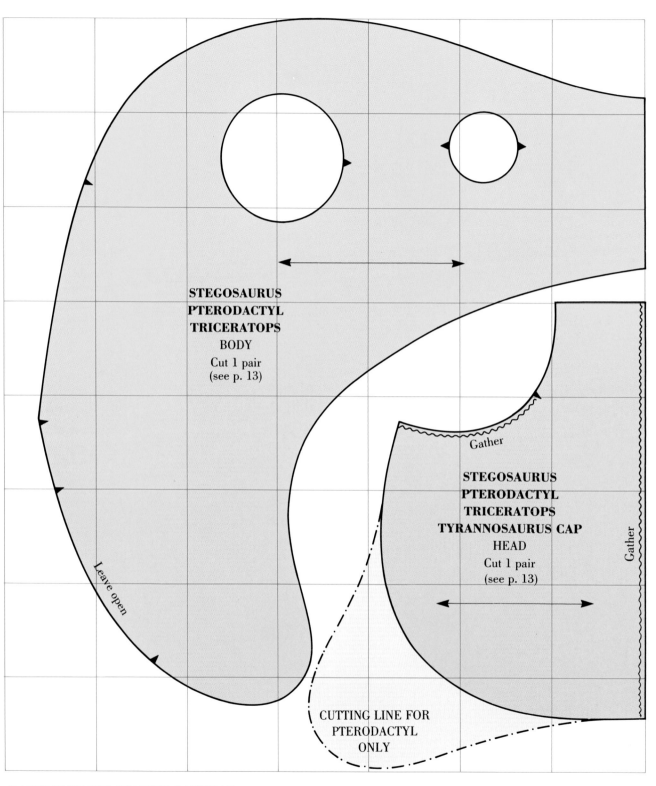

STEGOSAURUS
PTERODACTYL
TRICERATOPS
BODY
Cut 1 pair
(see p. 13)

Leave open

Gather

STEGOSAURUS
PTERODACTYL
TRICERATOPS
TYRANNOSAURUS CAP
HEAD
Cut 1 pair
(see p. 13)

Gather

CUTTING LINE FOR
PTERODACTYL
ONLY

DAFT DINOSAURS CHARTED PATTERNS: 1 sq = 5 cm (2 in)

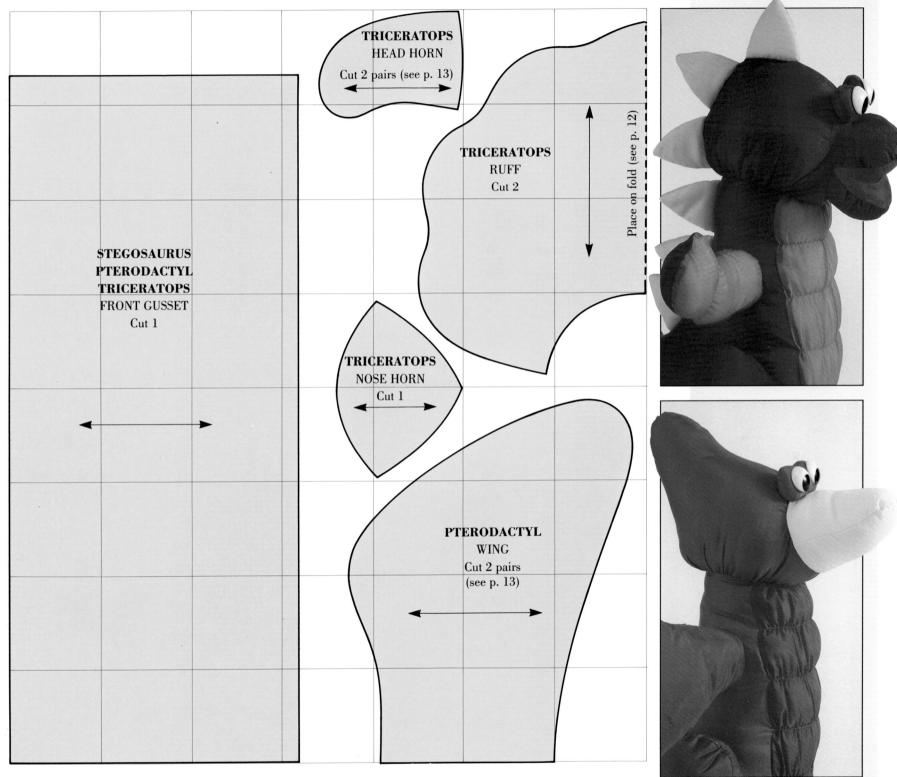

TRICERATOPS
HEAD HORN
Cut 2 pairs (see p. 13)

TRICERATOPS
RUFF
Cut 2

Place on fold (see p. 12)

STEGOSAURUS
PTERODACTYL
TRICERATOPS
FRONT GUSSET
Cut 1

TRICERATOPS
NOSE HORN
Cut 1

PTERODACTYL
WING
Cut 2 pairs
(see p. 13)

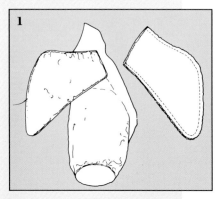

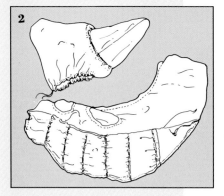

You Will Need:

40 cm (¹/₂ yd) of 150 cm (60 in)
wide purple shell suit nylon
20 cm (¹/₄ yd) of 150 cm (60 in)
wide cerise shell suit nylon
A scrap of yellow shell suit nylon
20 cm (¹/₈ yd) of 150 cm (60 in)
wide fine Terylene wadding
A pair of 24 mm (1 in) diameter
safety toy eyes
A scrap of iron-on interfacing
250 g (9¹/₂ oz) of toy stuffing
Matching sewing threads

Cutting Out:

*Enlarge the charted patterns on
pp. 24, 26–27 to 200% (either
using a photocopier or by charting
on to graph paper – see p. 12).
Cut the front gusset, tail gusset,
soles, and one pair of wings from
cerise, and the beak pieces from
yellow. Also cut a pair of wing
pieces, and both beak pieces, from
wadding. Cut all the remaining
pieces from purple.*

*Take 6 mm (¹/₄ in) seam turnings
throughout.*

PTERODACTYL

1 *Make up the legs and sew to
the body as for the stegosaurus
(step 1, p. 22). With contrasting
wing pieces right sides together,
sandwich them between two pieces
of wadding and sew all round,
leaving the straight edges open.
Turn to the right side and sew into
armholes as for stegosaurus (step
2, p. 22).*

2 *Make up the gusset and sew to
the body, then sew the body pieces
together, as for the stegosaurus,
omitting the fins (steps 3–5,
pp. 22–23). Pin a wadding piece
to the wrong side of each beak
piece, then sew the beak pieces
together, leaving the base edges
open. Following the instructions
for the stegosaurus, make up the
head, omitting fins, and insert the
beak in the opening as directed
for the upper and under jaws
(steps 6–8, p 23). Sew the head to
the body, then turn to the right
side and stuff, leaving wings
unstuffed. Ladder stitch opening
(see p. 20) and make up the
eyes as for the stegosaurus (steps
9–10, p. 24).*

▼ *Keep your eye open for modern
fabrics such as the almost
flourescent shell suit nylon used to
make these delicious dinosaurs.
Many of the new textiles are
suitable for soft-toy making and
will inspire original and
innovative creations.*

TRICERATOPS

1 *Make up the body and head as for the stegosaurus, omitting the fins (steps 1–8, pp. 22–23). Take the ruff pieces right sides together and sandwich them between the two pieces of wadding. Sew all round the wavy edge, leaving the base edge open. Turn ruff to the right side, fit inside the neck opening on the body and tack the neck edges together, matching the side edges of the ruff with the front gusset seams and the arrowhead on the ruff with the back seam of the body. Now fit and tack the head inside the opening as for stegosaurus, then sew the head, ruff and body together and remove tacking.*

2 *Turn to the right side, stuff, join opening and make up the eyes as for the stegosaurus (steps 9–10, p. 24). Catch the inside layer of ruff fabric to the back head seam with a few stitches to make the ruff stand upright. Pin wadding to the wrong side of the nose horn piece, work a row of stitching 6 mm (¹/4 in) up from the base edge, then fold in half and join side seam. Turn to right side, stuff lightly, then sew to upper jaw, folding under and sewing along stitched base line. Take head horn pieces right sides together and sandwich them between two pieces of wadding. Sew together, leaving the base edges open, then sew round base as for the nose horn. Turn horns to right side, stuff, then position and sew them in place as before.*

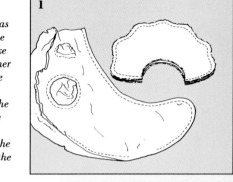

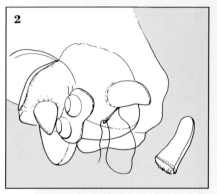

You Will Need:
40 cm (¹/2 yd) of 150 cm (60 in) wide green shell suit nylon
20 cm (¹/4 yd) of 150 cm (60 in) wide yellow shell suit nylon
Scraps of erise and orange shell suit nylon
Fine Terylene wadding
A pair of 24 mm (1 in) diameter safety toy eyes
A scrap of iron-on interfacing
250 g (9¹/2 oz) of toy stuffing

Cutting Out:
Enlarge the charted patterns on pp. 24, 26–27 to 200% (either using a photocopier or by charting on to graph paper – see p. 12). Cut the front gusset, tail gusset, soles, one pair of arms and one ruff piece from yellow, the mouth pieces from cerise and the nose horn and head horn pieces from orange. Also cut a pair of ruff pieces and matching horn pieces from wadding. Cut all the remaining pieces from green.

Take 6 mm (¹/4 in) seam turnings throughout.

BASIC TEDDY

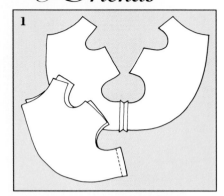

1 *Join front and back body pieces together in pairs along the seam A–B, then press the seam open.*

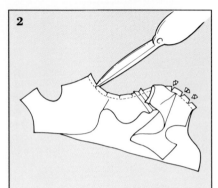

2 *Sew the top edge of each leg into the leg opening on each body half, matching points B, then clip the seam turnings (see p. 19).*

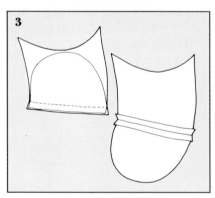

3 *Sew the paw and inner arm pieces together, then press the seams open.*

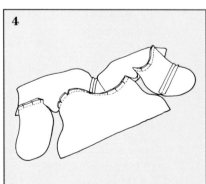

4 *Sew the top edge of the inner arm pieces into the front body arm openings, and the top edge of the outer arm pieces into the back body arm openings. Clip the seam turnings.*

You Will Need:
30 cm (¹/₃ yd) of 115 cm (45 in) wide main fabric
Oddments of contrast fabric
Pair of 10.5 mm (³/₈ in) diameter safety toy eyes
Embroidery thread
250g (9¹/₂ oz) of toy stuffing
Matching sewing threads

Cutting Out:
Trace off the same-size patterns on pp. 32–35, then mark out the snout, paw and sole pieces on the contrast fabric and the remaining pieces on the main fabric. Cut out.

Take 6 mm (¹/₄ in) seam turnings throughout.

▼ *No soft toy book is complete without the most cherished toy of all – the teddy bear. Use traditional fabrics such as tartan, felt and printed cotton or create more unusual characters with denims, laces and brocades.*

5 *With the front and back body and arm pieces right sides together, and the leg folded in half, sew from the neck edge, round the arm, down the side of the body, and along the front seam of the leg.*

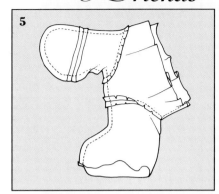

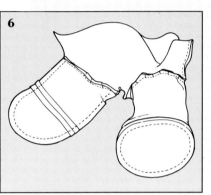

6 *Tack and sew a sole piece to the base of each leg, matching the arrowheads on the sole to the leg seam and leg arrowhead. Remove the tacking.*

7 *Join the body halves together along the centre front and centre back seams, leaving the neck edge open.*

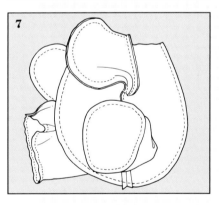

8 *Sew the ear pieces together in pairs, leaving the base edges open. Trim the seams (see p. 19), turn the ears through to the right side, then stuff them lightly.*

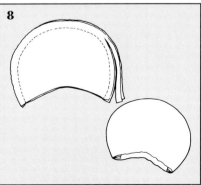

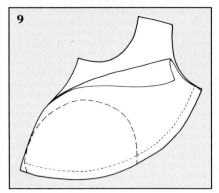

9 *Sew the front and back head side pieces together, inserting an ear in each seam between the arrowheads.*

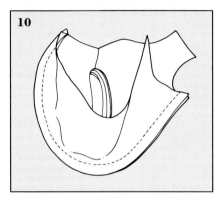

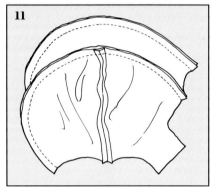

10 *Sew one of the head side pieces to one side of the head gusset, matching the head seam to the arrowhead on the gusset.*

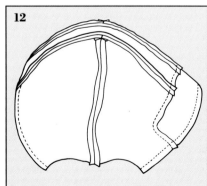

11 *Now sew the other head side piece to the opposite side of the head gusset as before.*

12 *Sew the snout piece to the front opening in the head, matching arrowheads, then sew the front head and snout seam.*

TEDDY BEARS AND FRIENDS SAME-SIZE PATTERNS

Enlarge the patterns on pp. 32–35 to 200% on a photocopier for Tartan Ted (p. 36) and reduce to 50% for Blanket Bunny and Blanket Bear (p. 39).

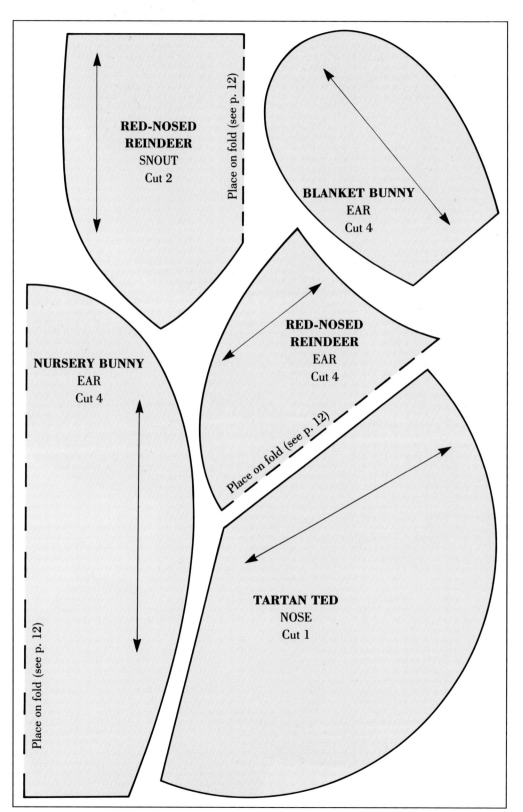

RED-NOSED REINDEER
SNOUT
Cut 2

Place on fold (see p. 12)

BLANKET BUNNY
EAR
Cut 4

RED-NOSED REINDEER
EAR
Cut 4

NURSERY BUNNY
EAR
Cut 4

Place on fold (see p. 12)

Place on fold (see p. 12)

TARTAN TED
NOSE
Cut 1

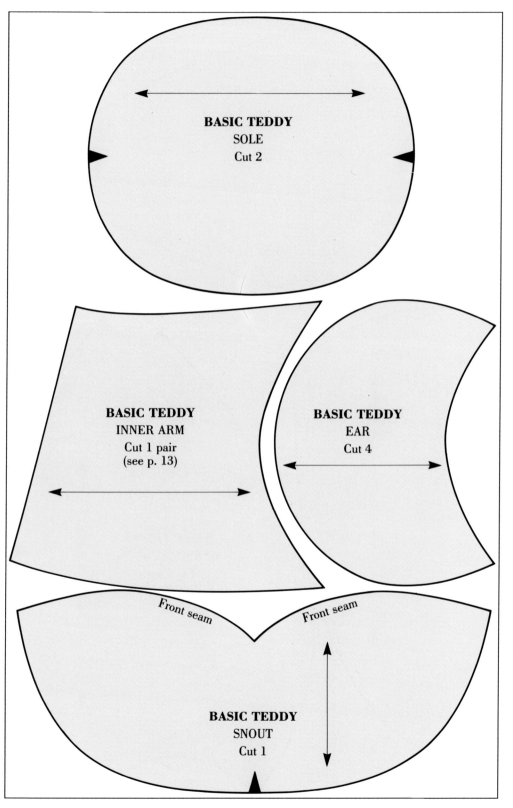

BASIC TEDDY
SOLE
Cut 2

BASIC TEDDY
INNER ARM
Cut 1 pair
(see p. 13)

BASIC TEDDY
EAR
Cut 4

Front seam   Front seam

BASIC TEDDY
SNOUT
Cut 1

13 *Turn the head to the right side and fix the eyes in the positions marked (see pp. 14–15).*

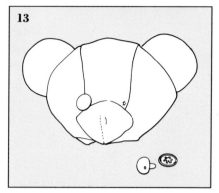

14 *Insert the head into the neck opening of the body. Matching side and front seams of head and body, tack and sew together along the neck edge, leaving the back of the neck open.*

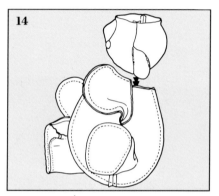

15 *Turn through to the right side and then stuff the head and body firmly. Ladder stitch the back neck opening closed (see p. 20).*

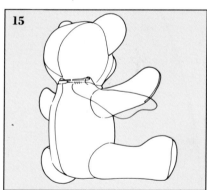

16 *Using double embroidery thread and a long needle, work a triangle of three straight stitches for nose, then fill in with satin stitch. Work the mouth with three long straight stitches. Fasten off the ends of the thread at the back of the neck.*

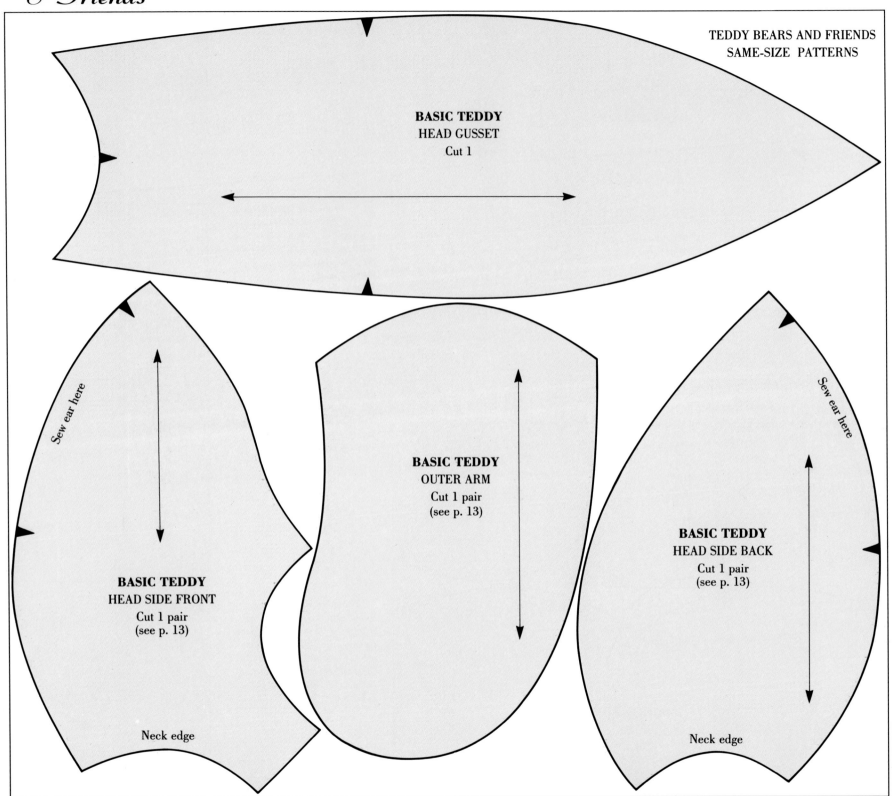

**TEDDY BEARS AND FRIENDS
SAME-SIZE PATTERNS**

BASIC TEDDY
HEAD GUSSET
Cut 1

Sew ear here

BASIC TEDDY
HEAD SIDE FRONT
Cut 1 pair
(see p. 13)

Neck edge

BASIC TEDDY
OUTER ARM
Cut 1 pair
(see p. 13)

Sew ear here

BASIC TEDDY
HEAD SIDE BACK
Cut 1 pair
(see p. 13)

Neck edge

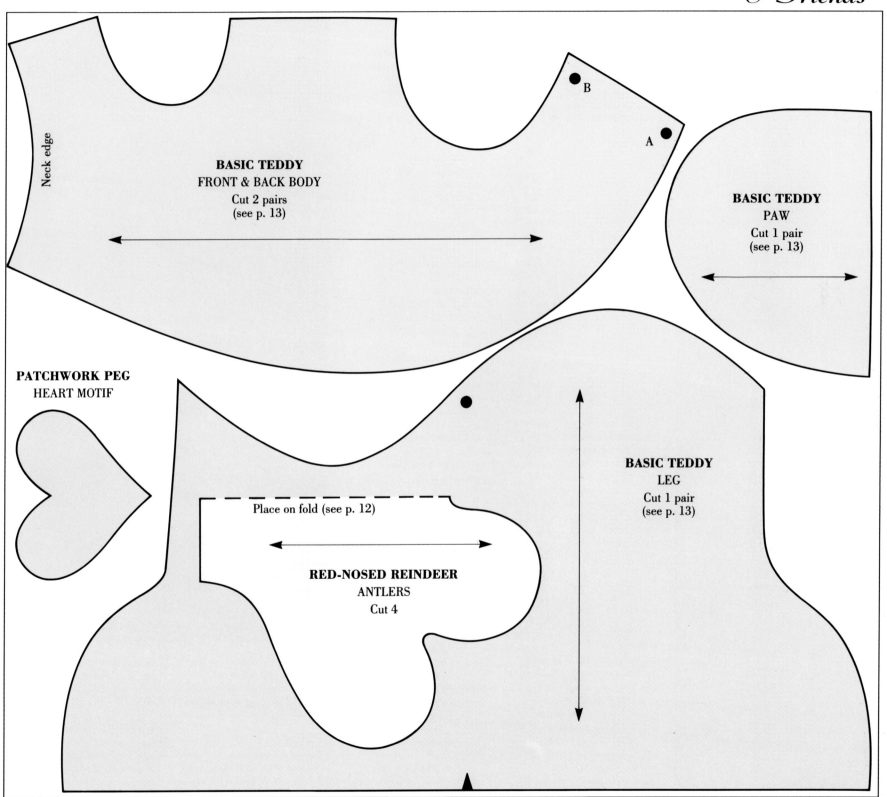

Neck edge

B

A

BASIC TEDDY
FRONT & BACK BODY
Cut 2 pairs
(see p. 13)

BASIC TEDDY
PAW
Cut 1 pair
(see p. 13)

PATCHWORK PEG
HEART MOTIF

BASIC TEDDY
LEG
Cut 1 pair
(see p. 13)

Place on fold (see p. 12)

RED-NOSED REINDEER
ANTLERS
Cut 4

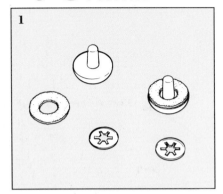

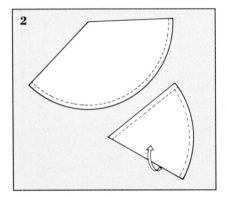

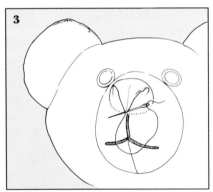

TARTAN TED

1 *Make up the bear, following the instructions for the basic teddy (pp. 30–33). Cut out two 24 mm (1 in) diameter circles of felt, then cut out a hole in the centre of each and slip over the eye shafts. Fix the eyes in place on the head (see pp. 14-15).*

2 *Embroider the mouth with double thread. Work a row of stitching 6 mm ($^1/4$ in) in from the curved edge of the nose, then join the straight edges, taking a 6 mm ($^1/4$ in) seam turning, to form a cone and turn through to the right side.*

3 *Lightly stuff the tip of the nose cone, then pin in place on the snout, placing the nose seam in line with the snout seam. Turn under the raw edge along the stitching line, and handsew in place. Fold down the tip of the cone and sew it to the base of the nose to form nostrils. Tie the ribbon round the neck in a bow.*

You Will Need:
1 m ($1^1/8$ yd) of 137 cm (54 in) wide wool tartan
Oddments of blue suedette
Scraps of black satin and yellow felt
Pair of 24 mm (1 in) diameter amber safety toy eyes
Black cotton perlé embroidery thread
1.30 m ($1^1/2$ yd) of 35 mm ($1^1/2$ in) wide green satin ribbon
1.2 kg ($2^1/2$ lb) of toy stuffing
Matching sewing threads

Cutting Out:
Photocopy the basic teddy pattern pieces on pp. 32–35, enlarging them to 200%. Cut out the snout, paw and sole pieces from suedette and the remaining pieces from tartan, matching the checks where possible. Cut the nose piece from satin.

Take 12 mm ($^1/2$ in) seam turnings throughout, trimming each seam after sewing (see p. 19).

BROCADE BELLE

1 *Make up the bear, following instructions for the basic teddy (pp. 30–33), omitting the eye and nose instructions, but working the mouth with double stranded cotton as before. Sew buttons securely in place for the eyes. Cut a 4 cm ($1^1/2$ in) diameter circle of silk for the nose and make up, following the fabric ball instructions (see p. 16). Sew the nose on to the snout.*

You Will Need:
30 cm ($^1/3$ yd) of 115 cm (45 in) wide cream brocade
Oddments of cream panne velvet
A scrap of pink silk
Two 1 cm ($^3/8$ in) diameter pearl buttons
Pink stranded embroidery thread
80 cm ($^7/8$ yd) of 15 mm ($^5/8$ in) wide pink satin ribbon
70 cm ($^3/4$ yd) of 3 mm ($^1/8$ in) wide pink satin ribbon

15 x 137 cm (6 x 54 in) strip of pink nylon net
Small wine red fabric rosebud
250 g ($9^1/2$ oz) of toy stuffing
Matching sewing threads

Cutting Out:
Cut out the snout, paw, sole and one pair of ear pieces from velvet fabric, and the remaining pieces from brocade.

▲ *Do not be afraid to sew lace and silky brocades to make teddies made of the finest materials. Seek out the most fragrant of pot pourris in place of stuffing for Scented Beau and create a delightful companion to sit on your dressing table. Brocade Belle makes an exquisite wedding present for any teddy lover.*

2 *Fold the net in half along its length and work a gathering thread close to the folded edge (see p. 20). Draw up to measure 35 cm (14 in). Even out the gathers, then pin centrally to the wide ribbon and sew in place, stitching close to the ribbon's edge. Separate the two layers of net and tie the skirt round the waist, making a bow at the back.*

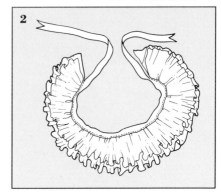

3 *Tie the narrow ribbon round the neck in a bow, and trim with the rosebud, sewn securely to the knot.*

SCENTED BEAU

1 *Make up the bear, following the instructions for the basic teddy (pp. 30–33), sewing the seams with a small zigzag stitch and trimming each seam after sewing (see p. 19). Stuff the finished bear with pot pourri, padding it out further with the toy stuffing pushed into the centre of the body and head. Omit stuffing from the ears, and work the features as for Brocade Belle*

2 *Tie wide ribbon round the neck in a bow. Twist the flower stems together and wrap with bias binding, holding in place with a little glue. Cut the narrow ribbon in half, then cut one of these pieces in half again. Tie the two shorter pieces round the posy, then tie the longer piece on top in a bow. Sew the posy securely in place on one paw.*

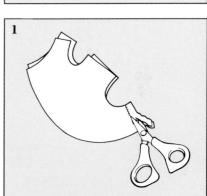

You Will Need:
30 cm (1/3 yd) of 115 cm (45 in) wide cream lace or embroidered net
Oddments of cream satin and fusible interfacing
A scrap of pink silk
Two 1 cm (3/8 in) diameter pearl buttons
Pink stranded embroidery cotton
40 cm (1/2 yd) of 6 mm (1/4 in)

wide pink satin ribbon
70 cm (3/4 yd) of 3 mm (1/8 in) wide pink satin ribbon
A short length of green bias binding
A few wine red silk roses and rosebuds
Clear adhesive
100 g (4 oz) of toy stuffing
250 g (9 1/2 oz) of pot pourri

Cutting Out:
Fuse the interfacing onto the back of the cream satin. Cut out the snout, paw, sole and one pair of ear pieces from interfaced satin, and the remaining pieces from lace.

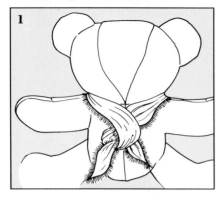

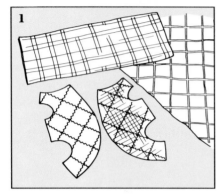

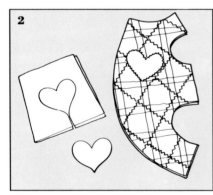

DENIM DAN

1 Make up the bear, following instructions for the basic teddy (pp. 30–33). Fray the edges of the checked fabric square, then dab a little glue at each corner to prevent further fraying. Fold diagonally and tie round the neck with a double knot at the back.

PATCHWORK PEG

You Will Need:
Small amounts of co-ordinating printed cotton fabrics
Oddments of blue denim shirting
Scraps of red cotton fabric and iron-on bonding web
30 cm (¹/₃ yd) of 90 cm (36 in) wide iron-on quilting interfacing
Pair of 10.5 mm (³/₈ in) diameter black safety toy eyes
Red cotton perlé embroidery thread
250 g (9¹/₂ oz) of toy stuffing
Matching sewing threads

Cutting Out:
Cut out the snout, paw and sole patterns from denim, and the remaining pieces from the mixture of printed fabrics. Also cut matching pieces of quilting interfacing to back each of the printed cotton pieces.

1 Fuse the quilting interfacing to the back of the printed cotton pieces and, using a small machine zigzag stitch, quilt over the printed lines.

2 Fuse the bonding web to the back of the red cotton fabric, then trace off the heart motif and transfer to the backing paper. Cut out the motif, remove the paper, position on the left front body piece and fuse in place. Appliqué round the edges with a narrow machine zigzag stitch. Make up the patchwork bear following the instructions for the basic teddy (pp. 30–33).

You Will Need:
30 cm (¹/₃ yd) of 115 cm (45 in) wide denim
Oddments of honey needlecord
35 cm (14 in) square of red/black woven check fabric
Pair of 10.5 mm (³/₈ in) diameter black safety toy eyes
Brown cotton perlé embroidery thread
250 g (9¹/₂ oz) of toy stuffing
Clear adhesive
Matching sewing threads

Cutting Out:
Cut out the snout, paw and sole pieces from needlecord, and the remaining pieces from denim.

BLANKET BEAR

You Will Need:
Oddments of wool coating
Scraps of felt
Two 12 mm ($^1/_2$ in) diameter buttons
Red cotton perlé embroidery thread
50 g (2 oz) of toy stuffing
Sewing thread to match felt

Cutting Out:
Photocopy the pattern pieces on pp. 32–35, reducing them to 50%. Cut out the snout, paw, sole and one pair of ear pieces from felt, and the remaining pieces from wool.

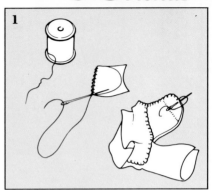

1 *Assemble both halves of the body in the same order as the basic teddy, but join wool pieces with wrong sides together and work blanket stitch over the raw edges with cotton perlé. Sew the felt paws to the arms by joining the pieces with right sides together and oversewing the edges with sewing thread. Similarly, sew the soles in place by turning the body wrong side out and oversewing as for the paws.*

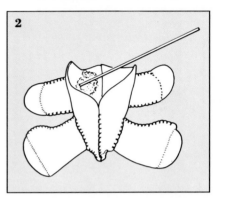

2 *Stuff the arms and legs before joining the body halves along the centre seams, then stuff the body firmly.*

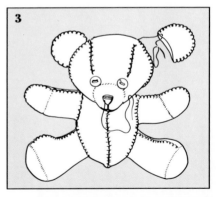

3 *Assemble the head in the same manner, omitting ears from side seams and oversewing felt snout in place as for the paws. Stuff the head firmly, then join to the body round the neck edge with blanket stitch. Stitch felt and wool ear pieces together in pairs, stuff lightly, then sew in place behind head side seams. Securely sew on the button eyes and embroider the mouth and nose with single thread.*

BLANKET BUNNY

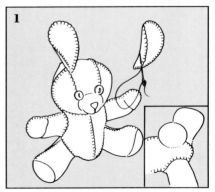

1 *Make up the body and head, following the instructions for the Blanket Bear. Stitch the felt and wool ear pieces together in pairs, fold in half and oversew across the base. Sew the ears to the head gusset seam, positioning them so the head side seams are in the centre of each ear. Make up the tail following the instructions for fabric balls (see p. 16) and sew it securely to the back of the bunny.*

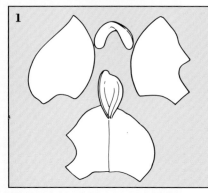

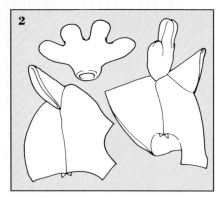

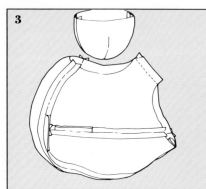

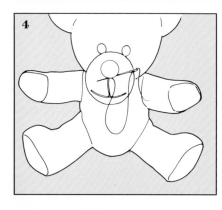

RED-NOSED REINDEER

You Will Need:
30 cm (¹/₃ yd) of 115 cm (45 in)
wide dark green needlecord
Oddments of Christmas print
cotton fabric
Scraps of red and cream
jersey velour
Pair of 10.5 mm (³/₈ in) black
safety toy eyes
Red cotton perlé
embroidery thread
80 cm (⁷/₈ yd) of 2 cm (³/₄ in)
wide gold lurex ribbon
A 24 mm (1 in) gold sleigh bell
250 g (9¹/₂ oz) of toy stuffing
Matching sewing threads

1 *Make up the body, following the instructions for the basic teddy (pp. 30–31). Sew the cord and print ear pieces together in pairs, leaving the base edges open. Trim the seams, turn the ear to the right side and fold in half. Join the head side pieces, inserting a folded ear in each seam, placing it centrally between the arrowhead markers for the teddy ear.*

2 *Sew the antler pieces together in pairs, leaving the base edges open. Turn antlers through to the right side and stuff them lightly. Sew one head side piece to the gusset, inserting an antler in the seam and positioning it so that the head side seam is in the centre of the antler. Repeat on the other side of the gusset.*

3 *Join the short front head seam. Now sew the dart on each snout piece, then sew both pieces together, leaving the base edges open. Turn the snout through to the right side, insert it into the front opening on head, matching snout seams with front head seam and arrowhead on gusset, and sew in place.*

4 *Fix the eyes on the head, then join and stuff the head and body as for the basic teddy (steps 14–15, p. 33). Embroider the mouth with double thread. Make up the nose, following the*

Cutting Out:
Use the teddy bear patterns on pp. 32–35 to cut out the pieces, substituting the reindeer ear and snout pieces on p. 32 for the teddy ear and snout. Cut out the paw, sole and one pair of ear pieces from the print fabric. Cut out the snout pieces from cream velour, and cut out the antler pieces from red velour, together with a 6 cm (2¹/₄ in) diameter circle for the nose. Cut out the remaining pieces from needlecord.

instructions for fabric balls (see p. 16), and sew it in place. Tie the ribbon round neck in a bow and sew the bell securely to the knot.

▲ *The basic teddy bear pattern is adapted to add two more irresistible characters to the hug. The bunny can be made in soft fabrics such as fleece and towelling for the nursery or in fresh, spring colours to create your own Easter Bunny.*

NURSERY BUNNY

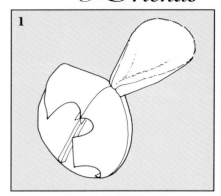

1 *Make up the body, following the instructions for the basic teddy (pp. 30–31). Sew the fleece and towelling ear pieces together in pairs, leaving the base edges open. Trim seams, then turn through to the right side. Join the front and back head side pieces. Sew one head side piece to the gusset, inserting an ear, folded in half, in the seam, and positioning so that the head side seam is in the centre of the ear. Repeat on the other side of the gusset.*

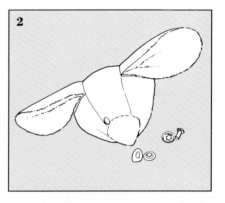

2 *Sew on the snout and make up the head as for the basic teddy (pp. 32–33). Fix the eyes, then fix the nose in the same manner at the top of the snout seam (see pp. 14–15). Join the head to the body and stuff, following steps 14 and 15 (p. 33) of the basic teddy.*

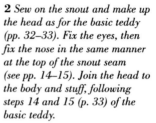

3 *Embroider the mouth with double thread. Catch the inside edge of the ears to the top of the head with a few stitches to make the ears stand up, and sew a small ribbon bow to the top of the head.*

4 *Work a row of machine stitching round the opening in the tail piece, then sew both tail pieces together. Turn through to the right side, stuff firmly, then sew the tail to the back of the bunny, following the stitching line round the opening.*

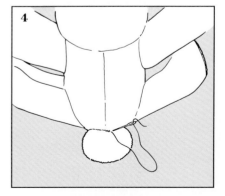

You Will Need:
30 cm (¹/₃ yd) of 150 cm (60 in) wide pink jersey fleece
Oddments of cream towelling
Pair of 10.5 mm (³/₈ in) diameter black safety toy eyes
A 21 mm (³/₄ in) pink flocked triangular safety toy nose
Pink soft embroidery cotton
20 cm (8 in) of 6 mm (¹/₄ in) wide pale blue satin ribbon
250 g (9¹/₂ oz) of toy stuffing
Matching sewing threads

Cutting Out:
Use the teddy bear patterns on pp. 32–35 to cut out the pieces, substituting the bunny ear piece on p. 32 for the teddy ear. Cut out the snout, paw, sole and one pair of ear pieces from towelling. Also cut out two 8 cm (3 in) diameter circles of towelling for the tail, cutting a 2 cm (³/₄ in) diameter circular hole from the centre of one piece. Cut the remaining pattern pieces from fleece.

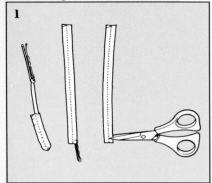

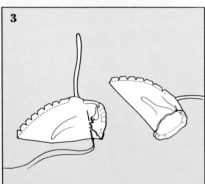

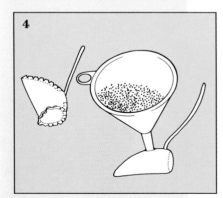

RING A RING O' MOUSIES

1 *Join the long sides of the tail strip. Cut a tiny notch 1 cm (³/8 in) in from one end and thread with the hair grip. Feed the hair grip through the tail and pull out at the opposite end to turn the tail to the right side. Use a needle to push in the raw edge at one end of the tail to neaten.*

2 *Fold the body piece in half and sew the curved back seam, inserting the tail in the seam where marked, and leaving the space marked open. Notch the seam turnings round the curved edge (see p. 18).*

3 *Clip within the seam turning around the base of the body (see p. 18). Feed the tail out through the body opening, then tack the base circle to the body's base edge, hand sew in place using backstitch and remove the tacking.*

4 *Notch the turning round the base circle, then turn the mouse through to the right side. Stuff the top third and the bottom third of the body with toy stuffing, then, using a funnel, fill the centre section with lavender. Plug with a little toy stuffing to stop the lavender falling out, then ladder stitch across the opening (see p. 20).*

You Will Need:
Oddments of three different
printed cotton fabrics
15 cm (6 in) squares of
felt in two colours
20 cm (¹/4 yd) of 90 cm (36 in)
wide extra fine
iron-on interfacing
A 30 x 15 cm (12 x 6 in) piece of
iron-on bonding web
40 cm (¹/2 yd) of 3 mm (¹/8 in)
wide satin ribbon in
each of two colours
12 tiny black glass beads, and
6 small pink pearl beads
100 g (4 oz) of toy stuffing
50 g (2 oz) of dried
lavender flowers
Funnel
Hot glue gun
Clear adhesive
A hair grip
Matching sewing threads

Cutting out:
Trace off the same-size pattern pieces on p. 45. Use the bonding web to fuse the felt squares to the two printed fabrics chosen for the mice. Cut out three pairs of arms and six ears from each of these pieces of fabric-backed felt. On the interfacing, draw six body pieces and six 5.5 cm (2¹/4 in) diameter circles for the base pieces. Fuse three body and three base pieces to each of the two printed fabrics and cut out. Mark the eye, ear, tail and arm positions on the right side of each piece with chalk. Also cut three 12 x 2.5 cm (4³/4 x 1 in) strips for the tails from each of the two printed fabrics, cutting the strips on the fabric's bias. For the pincushion, cut two 15 cm (6 in) diameter circles from the third printed fabric.

Take 6 mm (¹/4 in) seam turnings throughout.

5 *Sew black beads at the eye positions, fastening off the ends of the thread at the nose point, then sew a pink bead in place on the tip of the nose. Spread a thin line of clear adhesive along the straight edge of two ears and glue in place where marked. Also glue the top of a pair of arms to the sides of the body where marked. Make all six mice in this manner*

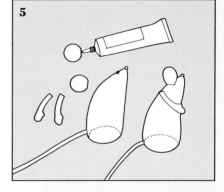

6 *Sew the pincushion circles together, leaving a 5 cm (2 in) space open in the seam. Notch turnings, then turn through to the right side and stuff firmly, filling the centre with the remaining lavender. Ladder stitch across the opening. Using the hot glue gun, position the mice evenly around the cushion and glue in place securely.*

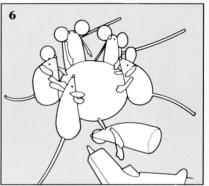

7 *Glue the felt palms of the hands together with clear adhesive. Cut each piece of ribbon into three equal pieces. Tie a ribbon bow 2.5 cm (1 in) in from the end of each tail, curve the tail round and glue the back of the bow in place on the back seam of the body.*

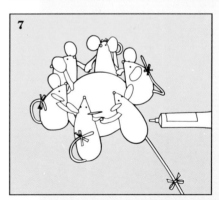

◀ *Who can resist such a charming circle of fairy mice? This decorative pin cushion makes a dainty dressing-table accessory while the mice will accompany you on all your subsequent toy-making projects*

Monster & Midget Mice

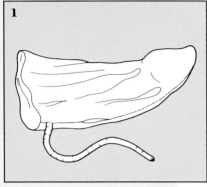

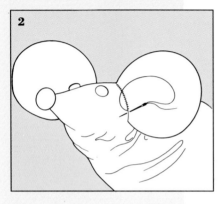

2 *Make fabric balls from the nose and eye circles (see p. 16) and sew in place. Place the needlecord and fleece ear pieces with right sides together and sandwich them between two layers of wadding. Make up the ears and sew them to the body, following instructions given in step 4 of Café Souris (p. 46). Also make up the arms as instructed in step 5 of Café Souris, and sew them to the body.*

You Will Need:
1.70 m (2 yd) of 150 cm (60 in)
wide pink cotton needlecord
Oddments of lilac polar fleece
Scraps of purple felt and
black satin
A small amount of thick
Terylene wadding
700 g (1¹/₂ lb) of toy stuffing
775 g (1³/₄ lb) of polystyrene
beanbag beads
Large safety pin
Matching sewing threads

MAMMOTH MOUSE

1 *Join the long sides of the tail piece and turn it through to the right side. Fold one short end of the wadding strip in half and pin the fold with the safety pin. Pad the tail with the wadding, using the pin to feed the strip through. Trim away any excess wadding from the ends of the tail, then gather round one end, draw it up tightly, pushing the raw edges inside the tail, and fasten off. Join the curved body seam, inserting the tail and leaving the marked space open. Sew the base circle to the base of the body. Turn the body to the right side through the opening. Stuff the top of the head down to the base of the ears with toy stuffing, then fill the remainder of the body with beads and ladder stitch across the opening (see p. 20).*

Cutting Out:
Following the pattern opposite, chart the pattern pieces on to graph paper (see p. 12), one square representing 12.5 cm (5 in). Add 12 mm (¹/₂ in) seam turnings to all three pattern pieces. From the needlecord cut out one body piece, two ear pieces, two pairs of arm pieces, and a 100 x 12 cm (40 x 4³/₄ in) strip for the tail. Mark the eye, ear, tail and arm positions on the right side of the body piece with chalk. Cut two ear pieces from polar fleece, a 12 cm (4³/₄ in) diameter circle of felt for the nose, and two 8 cm (3 in) diameter circles of satin for the eyes. From the wadding cut four ear pieces, and a 100 x 10 cm (40 x 4 in) strip to pad the tail.

Take 12 mm (¹/₂ in) seam turnings throughout.

▲ *A mouse full of beans and big enough to frighten off the bravest of elephants! His enormous arms will even stretch to give his companion a hug.*

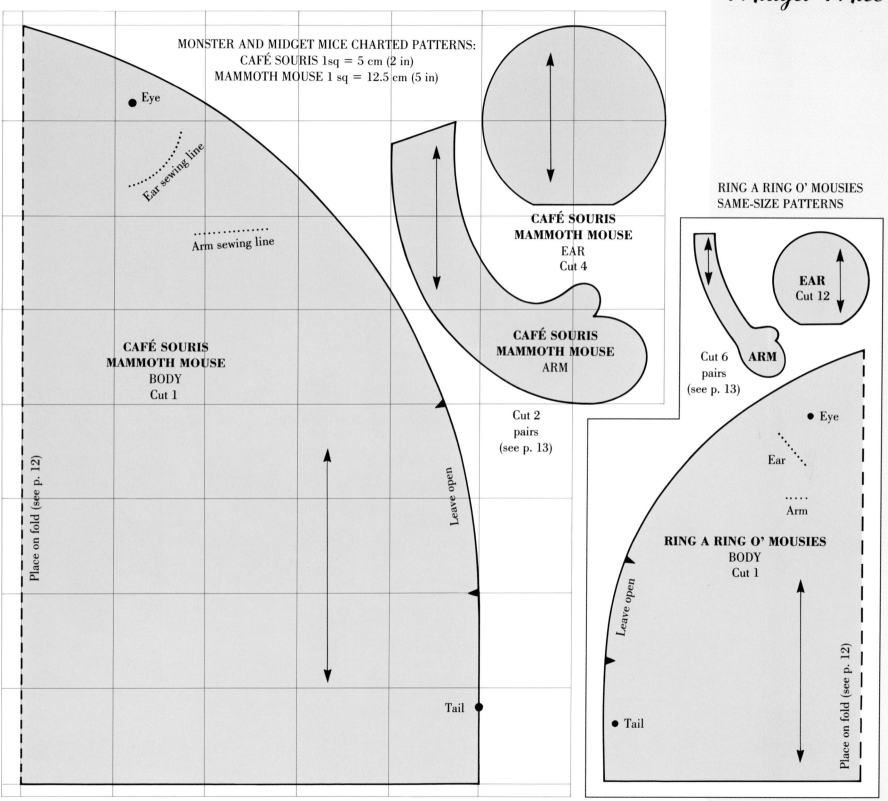

MONSTER AND MIDGET MICE CHARTED PATTERNS:
CAFÉ SOURIS 1 sq = 5 cm (2 in)
MAMMOTH MOUSE 1 sq = 12.5 cm (5 in)

• Eye

Ear sewing line

Arm sewing line

CAFÉ SOURIS
MAMMOTH MOUSE
BODY
Cut 1

Place on fold (see p. 12)

Leave open

Tail •

CAFÉ SOURIS
MAMMOTH MOUSE
EAR
Cut 4

CAFÉ SOURIS
MAMMOTH MOUSE
ARM

Cut 2
pairs
(see p. 13)

RING A RING O' MOUSIES
SAME-SIZE PATTERNS

EAR
Cut 12

Cut 6
pairs
(see p. 13)

ARM

• Eye

Ear

Arm

RING A RING O' MOUSIES
BODY
Cut 1

Leave open

• Tail

Place on fold (see p. 12)

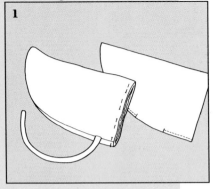

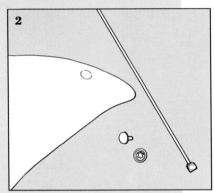

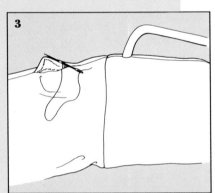

CAFÉ SOURIS

1 *Join the long sides of the tail. Gather round one end, draw up tightly and fasten off. Turn tail to the right side. Pin thick wadding to wrong side of fleece body piece, then fold in half with right sides of fleece together and sew curved back seam, inserting tail in seam where marked and ignoring the opening in the back seam. Notch the curved seam (see p. 18) and turn body through to the right side. Sew the back seam on poplin lining piece, leaving the marked space open, and leave wrong sides out.*

2 *Using a knitting needle, make holes through the fleece and wadding at eye positions and fix the toy eyes securely in place (see pp. 14-15).*

3 *Fit the lining over the fleece body and pin them together round the base edge. Sew round the base, then turn the body to the right side through the opening in the lining. Ladder stitch across the opening (see p. 20), then push the lining up inside the fleece body.*

4 *Take the fleece and velvet ear pieces right sides together and sandwich them between two matching pieces of wadding. Sew all round, leaving the straight edges open. Notch turnings, then turn to right side and ladder stitch across opening. Sew the ears to the head where marked.*

You Will Need:
50 cm (¹/2 yd) of 150 cm (60 in) wide jade green polar fleece
A 55 x 45 cm (22 x 18 in) piece of cerise cotton poplin, and a matching piece of thick Terylene wadding
Oddments of cerise jersey panne velvet and thin Terylene wadding
20 cm (¹/4 yd) of 115 cm (45 in) wide pink and white spotted cotton fabric
A pair of 15 mm (⁵/8 in) diameter black safety toy eyes
Anti-fray fabric sealer
50g (2oz) of toy stuffing
Matching sewing threads

Cutting Out:
Following the charted pattern on p. 45, either enlarge to 200% on a photocopier, or chart on to graph paper (see p. 12), one square representing 5 cm (2 in). Add 6 mm (¹/4 in) seam turnings to all three pattern pieces. From the polar fleece cut one body piece, two ear pieces, two pairs of arm pieces, and a 40 x 5 cm (16 x 2 in) strip for the tail. Mark eye, ear, tail and arm positions on the right side of the body piece with chalk. From the thick wadding cut one body piece, and from the thin wadding cut four ear pieces. From the poplin cut one body piece, trimming off 2.5 cm (1 in) from the base edge. From the panne velvet cut two ear pieces and a 5 cm (2 in) diameter circle for the nose. From the spotted cotton cut a 15 x 10 cm (6 x 4 in) rectangle for the apron, rounding off the corners at each end of one long side by drawing round a cotton reel and trimming away the excess. Also cut a 60 x 5 cm (24 x 2 in) strip for the frill, and two 45 x 5 cm (18 x 2 in) strips for the waistband and bow.

Take 6 mm (¹/4 in) seam turnings throughout.

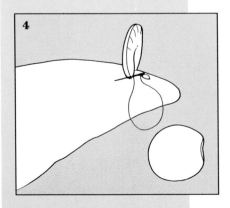

5 *Make a fabric ball from the nose circle (see p. 16) and sew in place on the body. Sew the arm pieces together in pairs, leaving the straight top edges open. Trim turnings and clip down to seam at base of thumb, then turn each arm through to the right side and stuff firmly. Ladder stitch across opening, then position and sew top edge to body along the marked lines.*

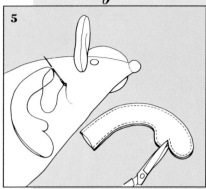

6 *To make the apron, with right side out fold the frill strip in half along its length and press flat. Work a gathering thread along the raw edge and draw it up to fit round the sides and base of the apron piece (see p. 21). Sew the frill and apron together, remove the gathering thread, then seal raw edges with anti-fray fabric sealer, or oversew raw edges together. When the glue is dry, press the seam lightly so that the turnings face inwards. Work a gathering thread across the top of the apron and draw it up to measure 10 cm (4 in).*

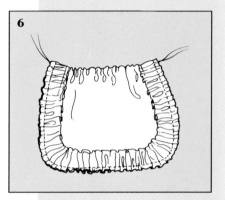

7 *With the wrong side of the apron together with the right side of the waistband piece, sew the apron centrally to one edge of the waistband. Fold under, and press down, 6 mm ($^1/_4$ in) on both long edges of the waistband, then fold it in half along its length and machine stitch the open edges together, stitching close to the edge. Fold under, and press down, 6 mm ($^1/_4$ in) all round the bow piece, fold it in half along the length and stitch the open edges as before, and across the ends.*

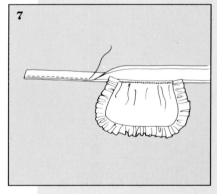

8 *Pin the apron on the mouse and sew the waistband ends together at the body back seam, Tie the bow piece into a bow and sew it securely over the waistband join to cover. Sew the tips of the hand together, then wrap the tail round the left arm and catch it in position with a few stitches.*

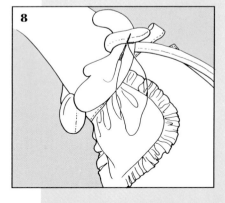

Spiders, Octopus & Fly

CLINGING SPIDER

You Will Need:

1m (1^1/$_8$ yd) of 115 cm (45 in)
wide purple towelling
Oddments of yellow, black
and white felt
20 cm (8 in) of black Velcro
13 cm (5 in) of red Russia braid
350 g (12 oz) of toy stuffing
Clear adhesive
Matching sewing threads

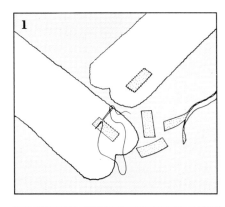

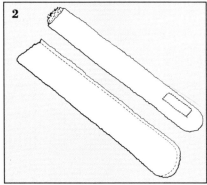

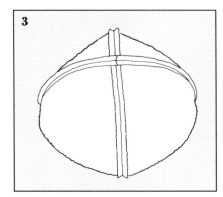

Cutting Out:
*Enlarge the clinging spider
patterns on p. 50 to 200% (either
by using a photocopier or by
charting on to graph paper – see
p. 12), cut out two pairs of body
pieces and eight legs from
towelling. Also from towelling cut
one 33 cm (13 in) diameter
circular base piece and two 20 cm
(8 in) diameter circular head
pieces, cutting out a 6 cm (2^1/$_4$ in)
diameter circular opening from
the centre of one head piece
only. For the eyeballs cut
two 10 cm (4 in)
diameter circles from
yellow felt.*

*Take 12 mm (^{1}/$_2$ in)
seam turnings
throughout.*

1 *Cut the Velcro into
four 5 cm (2 in)
lengths. Separate the
two sections of each
strip, then sew one
section to the right side
of each leg piece within the space
marked on the pattern.*

2 *Fold each leg in half with right
sides together. Sew down the side
seam and round the curved edge
of the foot, leaving the top edge of
the leg open. Turn through to
the right side and stuff leg
lightly.*

3 *With right sides together,
take the body pieces in pairs
and join each pair along the
side seam. Press the seam
open. Now join these two
pieces, with right sides
together, along the centre
seam. Press the seam open
as before.*

4 Fold the top of each leg flat, with the seam at one side edge, and pin with right sides together with the body within the spaces marked on the pattern, placing all the legs with looped Velcro strips facing upwards on one side, and all the legs with hooked Velcro strips facing downwards on the opposite side. Sew in place and remove the pins.

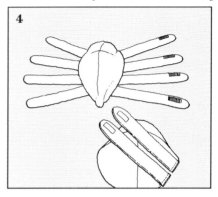

5 Sew the base piece to the body and legs, following the previous stitching line across top of legs, and leaving the space between the two front legs unsewn. Turn to the right side through this opening, stuff the body firmly, then ladder stitch the opening to close (see p. 20).

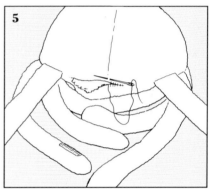

6 Sew round the head opening 12 mm (¹/₂ in) in from the cut edge to prevent it stretching. Sew the head pieces together, then trim the seam turning (see p. 19). Turn the head to the right side through the opening and stuff firmly.

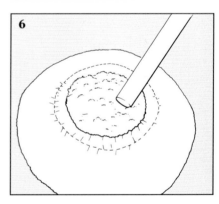

7 Position and sew head securely in place on body, following the line of stitching round the opening. Make up the eyeballs (see p. 16) and sew in position on the face, then glue 1 cm (³/₈ in) diameter circles of sealed black felt (see p. 17) in place on the eyes. Trace off the fang pattern and cut two pieces from white sealed felt. Glue in place, together with the braid mouth.

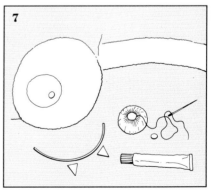

▲ Velcro attached to each leg gives this spider a very firm grip. You will not want to put him out of the window – but you will want to pick him up!

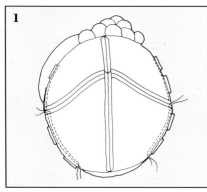

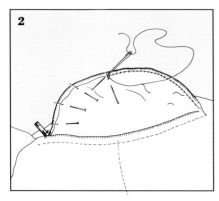

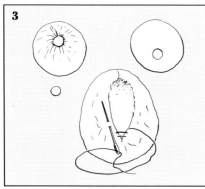

OCTOPUS BACKPACK

1 *Tack the wadding to wrong side of body and base pieces. Make up, following steps 1 to 4 of the clinging spider instructions (pp. 48–49). Now sew the front halves of the body and the base pieces together, leaving the space between the front legs unsewn as before. Insert the zip in opening.*

2 *Leaving the zip open, sew the remainder of the body and base together, then turn to right side through zip opening. Make up lining, leaving a 20 cm (8 in) space open as before when joining the body to the base piece. Fit lining inside octopus, turn under 12 mm (1/2 in) along both sides of opening, and handsew to inside of zip.*

3 *Sew nose pieces together, turn to right side through slit, stuff firmly and join opening. Make up eyes as for the spider and sew in place, together with the nose.*

Cutting Out:
Enlarge the octopus patterns on this page to 200% (either by using a photocopier or by charting on to graph paper – see p. 12). Cut out two pairs of body pieces, eight legs and two nose pieces from taffeta, cutting along the dotted line on one nose piece only. Also from taffeta cut a 33 cm (13 in) diameter circular base piece. From the chintz lining and from the wadding cut two pairs of body pieces and one base piece. For the eyeballs cut two 10 cm (4 in) diameter circles from lilac felt.

Take 12mm (1/2 in) seam turnings throughout.

You Will Need:
1 m (1 1/8 yd) of 115 cm (45 in) wide green waffle taffeta
60 cm (2/3 yd) of 115 cm (45 in) wide purple cotton chintz
40 cm (1/2 yd) of 150 cm (60 in) wide fine Terylene wadding
Oddments of lilac and black felt
20 cm (8 in) green nylon zip
20 cm (8 in) of black Velcro
100 g (4 oz) of toy stuffing
Clear adhesive
Matching sewing threads

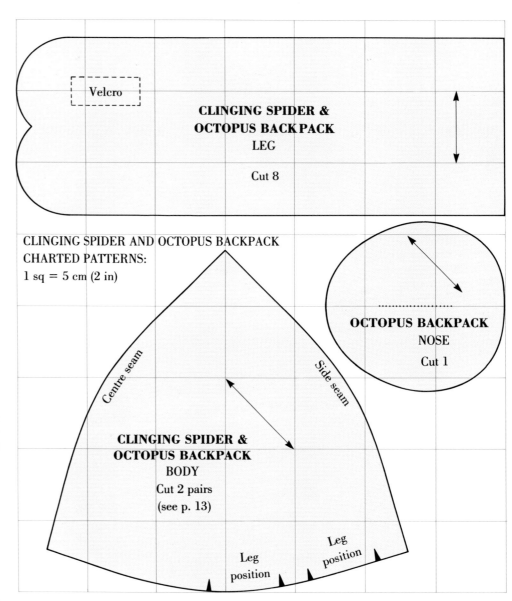

Velcro

CLINGING SPIDER & OCTOPUS BACKPACK LEG

Cut 8

CLINGING SPIDER AND OCTOPUS BACKPACK CHARTED PATTERNS:
1 sq = 5 cm (2 in)

OCTOPUS BACKPACK NOSE

Cut 1

Centre seam

Side seam

CLINGING SPIDER & OCTOPUS BACKPACK BODY

Cut 2 pairs
(see p. 13)

Leg position

Leg position

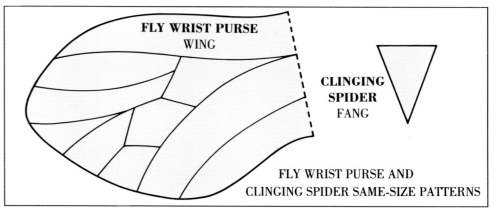

FLY WRIST PURSE WING

CLINGING SPIDER FANG

FLY WRIST PURSE AND CLINGING SPIDER SAME-SIZE PATTERNS

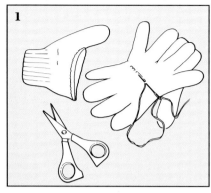

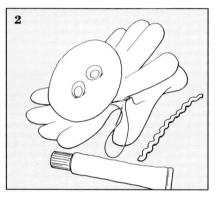

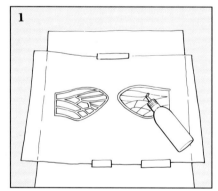

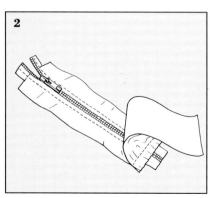

SPIDER GLOVE PUPPET

1 *Cut across one glove directly above the thumb and throw away the bottom half. Unravel a couple of rows of the knitting from the top half and thread the spare yarn through the open knit stitches to prevent any further unravelling. Stuff the fingers lightly, then, using the rest of the unravelled yarn, sew to the top of the remaining glove with the fingers pointing in the opposite direction.*

2 *Make up the body following step 6 of the clinging spider's head, and stuff firmly. Mark eye positions with chalk and fix eyes in place (see pp. 14–15). Sew the body to the glove, taking care to sew through the top layer of knitting only. Glue the braid in place to form the mouth.*

You Will Need:
Pair of purple knitted gloves
Oddment of purple towelling
Pair of 15 mm (5/8 in) diameter
safety joggle toy eyes
3.5 cm (1 1/2 in) of red
ricrac braid
Small amount of toy stuffing
Clear adhesive
Purple sewing thread

Cutting Out:
Cut two 12 cm (4 3/4 in) diameter circles of towelling for the body, cutting out a 4 cm (1 1/2 in) diameter circular opening from the centre of one piece only.

Take 12 mm (1/2 in) seam turnings.

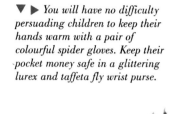

▼ ▶ *You will have no difficulty persuading children to keep their hands warm with a pair of colourful spider gloves. Keep their pocket money safe in a glittering lurex and taffeta fly wrist purse.*

FLY WRIST PURSE

1 *Trace off the wing pattern on p. 50 and transfer it twice onto a sheet of white paper, reversing the tracing once to make a pair. Cover with the plastic and hold in place with a few pieces of sticky tape. Draw over the design lines with the glitter paint, then leave to set completely. Cut out the wings.*

2 *Fold the zip gusset pieces in half and sew the folded edges to the sides of the zip. Now sew one end of the side gusset piece to one end of the zip gusset.*

You Will Need:
Oddments of purple/green
shot taffeta
15 cm (6 in) square of clear
plastic, cut from a ring
binder envelope
Scrap of black/silver lurex jersey

25 cm (10 in) of 25 mm (1 in)
wide black nylon webbing
10 cm (4 in) purple nylon zip
5 cm (2 in) of black Velcro
Green glitter fabric paint
Small amount of toy stuffing
Matching sewing threads

Cutting Out:

From taffeta cut two 12 x 4 cm (4³/4 x 1¹/2 in) zip gusset pieces, one 12 x 4.5 cm (4³/4 x 1³/4 in) side gusset piece, two 8 cm (3¹/4 in) diameter circular underside pieces, and two 10 cm (4 in) diameter circular topside pieces. For the eyes cut two 6 cm (2¹/4 in) diameter circles from lurex jersey.

Take 6 mm (¹/4 in) seam turnings throughout.

3 *Sew the remaining ends of the gusset pieces together to form a band, then neaten the raw fabric edges with a zigzag stitch.*

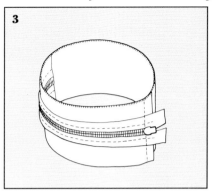

4 *Neaten the raw edges of the side pieces, then gather round the edge of each topside piece and draw up to fit the underside pieces. Tack and sew the top and underside pieces together, stuffing lightly, then remove the tacking.*

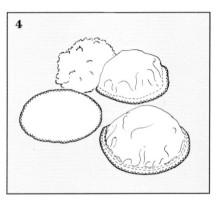

5 *Tack and sew one side piece to the gusset band, inserting a wing, positioned in the centre of the zip gusset, in the seam. Work other wing seam in the same way. Remove tacking and turn the purse through to the right side.*

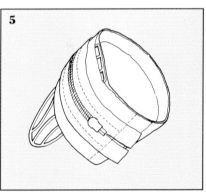

6 *Make up the eyeballs (see p. 16) and sew them to the front of the fly. Seal the cut ends of the webbing by holding them against a hot iron until the fibres melt. Sew the Velcro sections to each end of the webbing, placing one on the topside and the other on the underside. Handsew the purse in place in the centre of the wristband.*

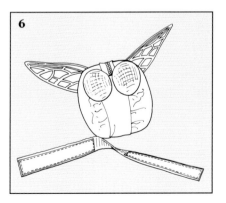

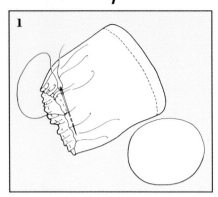

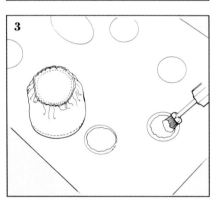

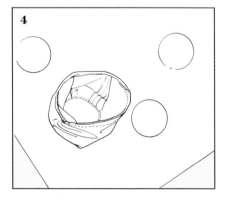

PAINT PALETTE

1 *Seal the short sides of the pocket rectangle with fabric sealer, then join and press the seam open. Hem the top edge by turning under 3 mm ($^1/_8$ in), then 1 cm ($^3/_8$ in), and sewing down close to the edge, leaving a 1.5 cm ($^5/_8$ in) space unsewn. Turn through to the right side, work a gathering thread round the unhemmed edge and draw up to fit round the circular base (see p. 20).*

2 *Sew the gathered edge to the base, then remove the gathering thread. Note that the raw edges of the fabric will be on the outside of the paint pocket. Make up the six coloured pockets.*

3 *Draw the position of each pocket on the right side of one PVC palette piece with a pencil. Spread latex adhesive inside this outline, and also over the gathered seam turning at the base of the pocket. Leave to become touch dry.*

4 *Position the pocket on the palette piece, folding under the pocket turning, and press in place. Working from the inside of the pocket, sew in place on the PVC by stitching over the seam line of the circular base.*

You Will Need:

40 x 30 cm (16 x 12 in) rectangle of lightweight foam-filled display board (or three layers of white mounting board glued together)
40 cm (^{1}/₂ yd) of 150 cm (60 in) wide white cotton-backed PVC
Oddments of cotton poplin in same colours as pixies
80 cm (^{7}/₈ yd) of 3 mm (^{1}/₈ in) wide white elastic
Craft knife
Latex adhesive
Clear adhesive
Anti-fray fabric sealer
Matching sewing threads

Cutting Out:

Enlarge the charted palette pattern on p. 57 to 200% (either by photocopier or by charting on to graph paper – see p. 12), then transfer it to the board and cut out the curved section and thumb hole with the knife. Cut out a pair of palette pieces from the PVC, together with two 2 cm (^{3}/₄ in) wide strips, one 140 cm (55 in) long and one 20 cm (8 in) long.

For the paint pockets cut a 25 x 10 cm (10 x 4 in) rectangle and a 6 cm (2^1/₂ in) diameter circle from each of the six colours of poplin.

Take 6 mm (^{1}/₄ in) seam turnings throughout

◀ *Use our troupe of paintpot pixies, housed in their own palette, to teach young children the names of the primary colours. Filled with lentils or plastic granules, they can be used as juggling beanbags by older children. Keep them company with a pair of immaculately coiffed brush boys.*

5 *Using a bodkin, thread the top hem of the pocket with 12 cm (4^3/₄ in) of elastic. Overlap ends by 1 cm (^{3}/₈ in) and sew together securely by hand, then machine stitch across the opening in the hem. Attach all the pockets to the palette in this manner.*

6 *Using latex adhesive, glue the long PVC strip round the outside edge of the card palette piece, folding over the excess equally to front and back, clipping round curves (see p. 18) and mitring corners. Repeat with the short strip round the inside of the thumb hole.*

7 *Spread latex adhesive over the back of the card palette, then position and press the PVC piece in place while the glue is still wet, smoothing out any air bubbles and working quickly.*

8 *Repeat on the other side of the palette. The latex adhesive will not glue PVC to itself, so gently lift up the PVC round the edge of the palette and spread the underside with a little clear adhesive. Press down the edges and leave to set.*

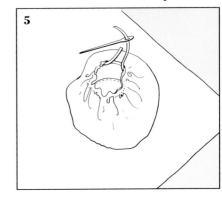

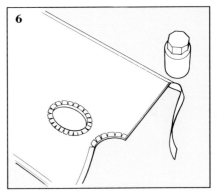

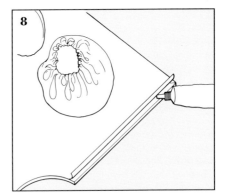

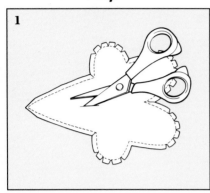

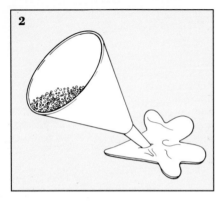

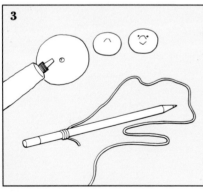

3 *Glue a bead in the centre of a jersey circle and stretch the fabric to fit over it. Gather the edge of the circle and draw up, stuffing it lightly to make a flat cushion shape. Using buttonhole twist, embroider eyes with French knots and a mouth with two straight stitches. Sew the head to the body, covering the opening. Blush the cheeks with coloured pencil. For hair, wind yarn round a pencil five times. Sew the loops together, then slip them off the pencil and sew them to the top of the head.*

PAINTPOT PIXIES

You Will Need:
Oddments of cotton poplin in red, orange, yellow, green, blue and purple
20 cm (8 in) lengths of double knitting yarn in the same colours
Scraps of white cotton jersey
30 cm (¹⁄₃ yd) of 90 cm (36 in) wide extra fine iron-on interfacing
Six 6 mm (¹⁄₄ in) white beads
Black buttonhole twist
360 g (12 oz) of PVC granules
Funnel
A small amount of toy stuffing
Coloured pencils
Clear adhesive
Matching sewing threads

Cutting Out:
Trace off the same-size body pattern on this page. For each pixie cut a piece of interfacing and a matching piece of poplin, both roughly twice the size of the pattern piece. Also cut out a 5 cm (2 in) diameter circle of jersey for each pixie's face.

1 *Fuse the interfacing to the wrong side of the poplin. Draw round the body pattern on to the interfacing with a pencil at one end of the fabric. Cut out roughly round the outline, then pin right sides together with the remaining fabric and, using a small stitch, sew all round the pencilled outline. Trim away fabric, 3 mm (¹⁄₈ in) from the sewing line, then clip and notch turnings (see p. 18). Cutting through the top layer of fabric only, cut the opening with a small pair of sharp scissors.*

2 *Carefully turn the body to the right side through the opening, using the rounded end of a pencil or paintbrush to turn out the arms, legs and hat. Fit a funnel in the opening and fill the body with about 60 g (2¹⁄₂ oz) of granules, leaving the hat unstuffed so that the body remains flexible. Oversew the edges of the opening together.*

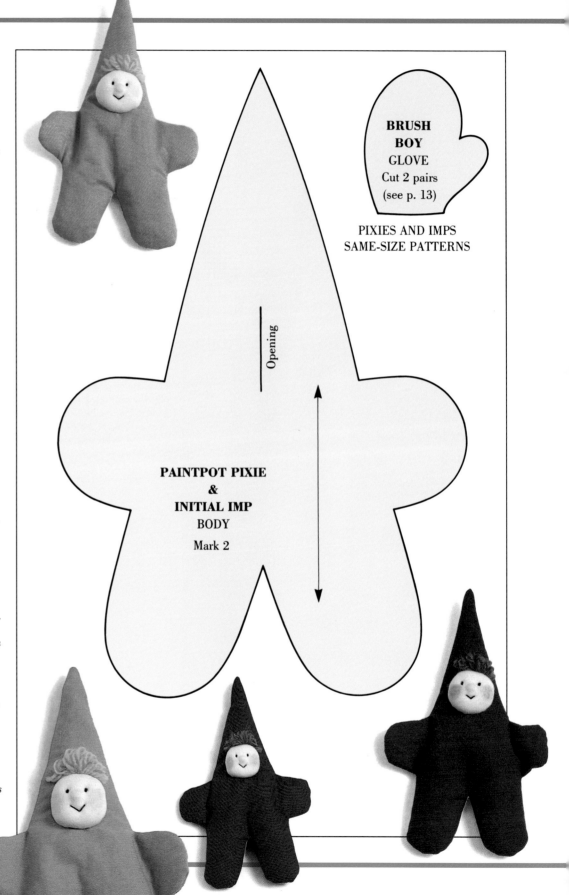

BRUSH BOY GLOVE
Cut 2 pairs
(see p. 13)

PIXIES AND IMPS
SAME-SIZE PATTERNS

Opening

PAINTPOT PIXIE & INITIAL IMP BODY
Mark 2

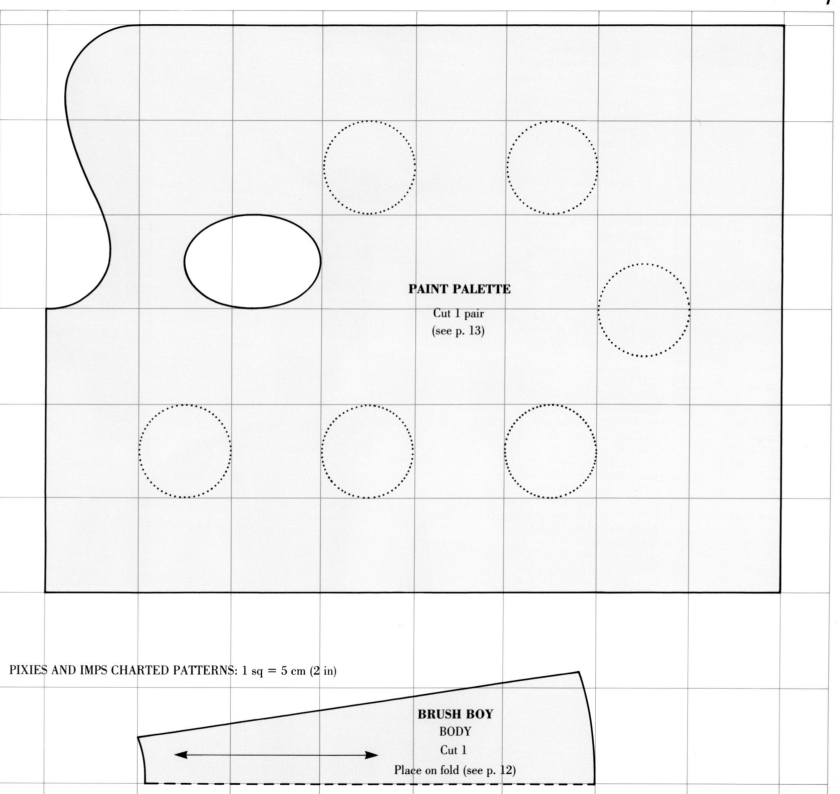

PAINT PALETTE

Cut 1 pair

(see p. 13)

PIXIES AND IMPS CHARTED PATTERNS: 1 sq = 5 cm (2 in)

BRUSH BOY

BODY

Cut 1

Place on fold (see p. 12)

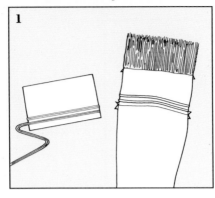

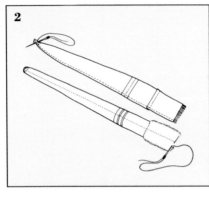

1 *Sew two lines of braid 1 cm and 2 cm (³/8 in and ³/4 in) in from one long side of the head piece. Join the body, head and hair pieces together, making sure that the fur pile runs upwards from the head piece.*

2 *Join the side seam, then gather round the base edge of the body, draw up tightly and fasten off. Turn through to the right side, then stuff the body and head sections firmly and the hair section lightly. Either gather up the top edge of hair, draw up tightly and fasten off, or fold the top edge flat so that the side seam runs down the centre back of the body, then ladder stitch across the top to close (see p. 20).*

BRUSH BOYS

You Will Need
For Each Brush Boy:
Oddments of black or tan satin, cream or chestnut fur fabric, red cotton jersey, white felt and silver lurex tissue fabric
A small amount of extra fine iron-on interfacing
Two plastic 'bendy' drinking straws
25 cm (10 in) of silver Russia braid
Black buttonhole twist
Two 6 mm (¹/4 in) diameter glue-on joggle eyes (optional)
30 g (1 oz) of toy stuffing
Hot glue gun
Matching sewing threads

Cutting Out:
Fuse the interfacing to the wrong side of the satin. For each Brush Boy, enlarge the charted body pattern on p. 56 to 200% (either by photocopier or by charting on to graph paper – see p. 12) and use to cut one piece from interfaced satin. Cut an 11 x 8 cm (4¹/2 x 3 in) rectangle of interfaced lurex tissue for the head, and an 11 x 6 cm (4¹/2 x 2¹/2 in) rectangle of fur fabric for the hair, having the fur pile running parallel to the shorter sides. Also cut two 6 x 3 cm (2¹/2 x 1¹/4 in) rectangles of jersey for the arms, having the most stretch running parallel to the shorter sides. Trace off the same-size glove pattern and cut two pairs from white felt, together with two 3.5 x 1 cm (1³/8 x ³/8 in) strips for the glove cuffs.

Take 6 mm (¹/4 in) seam turnings throughout.

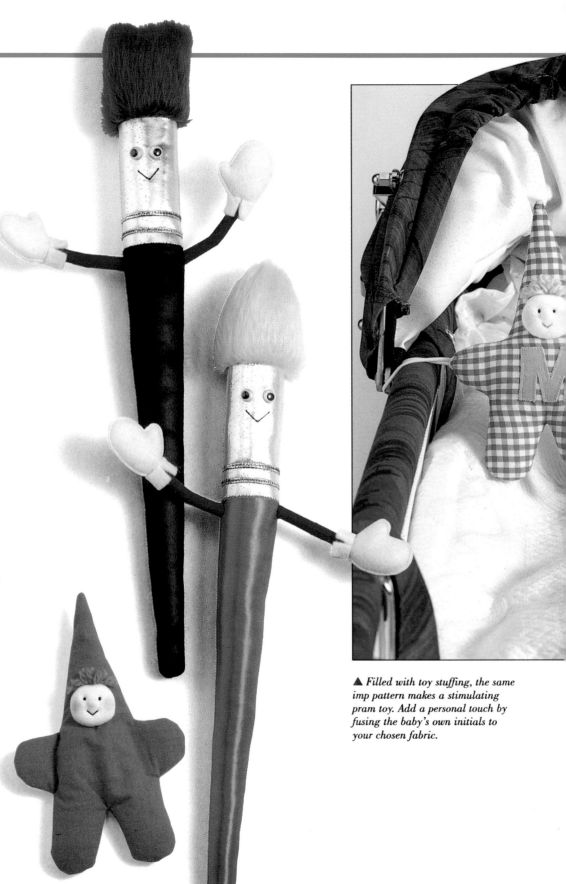

▲ *Filled with toy stuffing, the same imp pattern makes a stimulating pram toy. Add a personal touch by fusing the baby's own initials to your chosen fabric.*

3 *Embroider the mouth with two straight stitches, fastening off the ends of thread at the eye positions with French knots. If you are using joggle eyes, fix them in place over the eye knots, using the hot glue gun.*

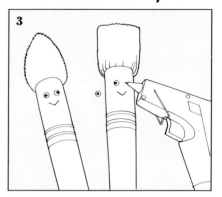

4 *Cut a 5 cm (2 in) length from each straw for the arms, having the pleated section in the centre. Join the long sides of each jersey piece, trim seam and turn through to the right side. Feed the straw down the sleeve, then squeeze a little glue from the gun into one end and push the fabric into the straw with scissor points, working quickly before the glue sets. Repeat at the other end.*

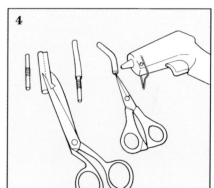

5 *Sew the glove pieces together in pairs, stitching close to the cut edge and leaving the straight top edge open. Stuff firmly, then gather round the top edge, insert an arm into the opening, draw up the thread to fit and sew the glove to the arm. Glue a cuff strip round the top edge, then sew the top of the arm securely to the side of the body. Repeat with the other arm, then bend the elbows into position.*

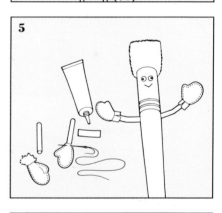

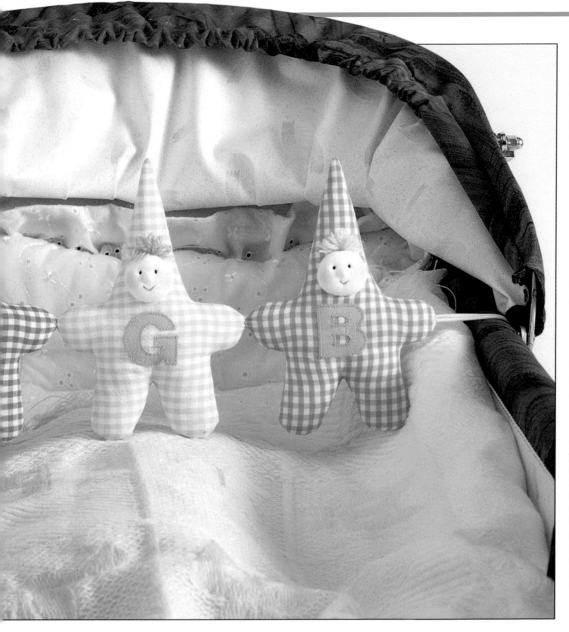

INITIAL IMPS

You Will Need:
Oddments of small check
gingham in three colours
Scraps of cotton poplin and
20 cm (8 in) lengths of double
knitting yarn in three colours to
contrast with the gingham
Scraps of white cotton jersey
20 cm (¼ yd) of 90 cm (36 in)
wide extra fine
iron-on interfacing
A small amount of iron-on
bonding web

Three 6 mm (¼ in) white beads
30 cm (⅓ yd) of thick white
cord elastic
Black and pink buttonhole twist
50 g (2 oz) of toy stuffing
Pink pencil
Clear adhesive
Matching sewing threads

Cutting Out:
Follow the cutting out instructions given for Paintpot Pixies (p. 55), substituting gingham for poplin.

1 *Fuse interfacing to the wrong side of the gingham. Draw round the body pattern on p. 56 on to the interfacing with a pencil at one end of the fabric. From a newspaper or magazine trace off the baby's initials and transfer the reversed images to the bonding web backing paper. Fuse the bonding web to the poplin fabrics, cut out the initials and remove the backing paper, then, position each on the initial interfaced gingham bodies and fuse in place. Appliqué the initials by working a narrow*

zigzag stitch over the cut edges. Finish making up the imps as for the pixies (p.55) and fill them with toy stuffing. Embroider the features, using black for eyes and pink for the mouth, and blush the cheeks with pink pencil. Sew the imps' hands together securely, then fold two 15 cm (6 in) lengths of elastic in half and knot the ends tightly. Sew these loops to the hands of the end imps and string the imps across the hood of a pram or carrycot.

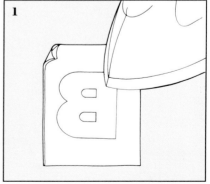

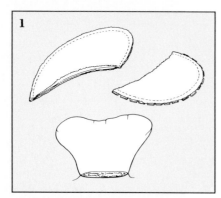

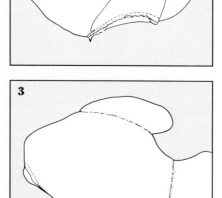

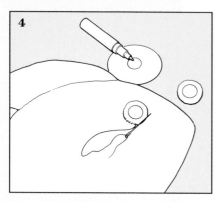

CLASSY CUSHIONS

1 *With the fin or tail pieces placed with right sides together, sandwich them between the matching pieces of wadding and sew together, leaving the base edges open. Clip, or notch, round the curved edges (see p. 18), then turn through to the right side.*

2 *Take one body piece and sew the fins and tail in place between the marked arrows, clipping turnings round curves.*

3 *Now sew the body pieces together, sewing over the fin and tail stitching lines and leaving the space open where marked. To provide a guide, work a row of stitching 6 mm (¹/₄ in) in from the cut edge on both sides of the opening. Turn the cushion through to the right side.*

4 *Stuff the body lightly, then ladder stitch the opening closed (see p. 20). Using satin for the fish, or the darker shade of moiré for the seahorse, cut out two 7 cm (2³/₄ in) diameter circles for the eyes. Draw a 2 cm (³/₄ in) spot in the centre of each satin piece, or a 1 cm (³/₈ in) spot in the centre of the moiré, with the felt pen. Leave to dry and fix the fabric paint as directed. Make up the circles into fabric eyeballs (see p. 16) and sew in place on the cushion.*

You Will Need
For Each Cushion:
30 cm (¹/₃ yd) for the fat fish or the seahorse, and 20 cm (¹/₄ yd) for the thin fish of 115 cm (45 in) wide moiré taffeta in main colour
A small amount of moiré taffeta in a darker shade
Scraps of cream or gold satin for the fish only
Oddments of thin polyester wadding
80 g (3 oz) for the fat fish or the seahorse, and 50 g (2 oz) for the thin fish of toy stuffing
Black fabric paint felt pen
Matching sewing threads

Cutting Out:
Either enlarge the shell, thin fish, fat fish and seahorse pattern pieces on p. 62 on to graph paper (see p. 12) or increase them to 400% on a photocopier. Marking arrows where the pieces join the body, cut along the dotted lines to separate the tail and fins from the body, then add a 6 mm (¹/₄ in) seam allowance all round each piece. Cut a pair of each pattern piece from moiré, cutting the body pieces from the lighter shade. Also cut a pair of the tail piece and each fin piece from wadding.

Take 6 mm (¹/₄ in) seam turnings throughout.

STARFISH CUSHION

You Will Need
For Each Cushion:
45 cm (½ yd) of 115 cm (45 in)
wide yellow silk-effect rayon
A 45 cm (18 in) square of
medium-weight Terylene
wadding
1.30 m (1½ yd) of old gold
silky ricrac braid
150 g (5 oz) of toy
stuffing
Air-vanishing
embroiderer's
marking pen
Matching sewing threads

Cutting Out:
*Enlarge the pattern piece on p. 62
on to graph paper (see p. 12) then
add a 6 mm (¼ in) seam
allowance all round. Cut a pair of
starfish from fabric and one
piece from wadding.*

*Take 6 mm (¼ in) seam
turnings throughout.*

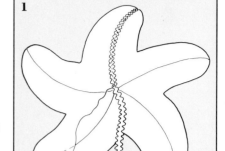

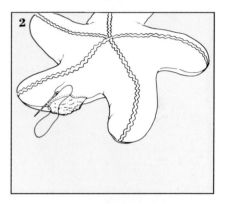

1 *Mark the braid sewing lines on
the right side of one piece of
fabric with pen, then pin this piece
on top of the wadding. Sew the
ricrac in place, following the lines
and stitching down the centre of
the braid. Start with one piece
taken from the centre point to the
tip of one leg. Now sew two more
pieces of braid in place, this time
starting at the tip of one leg,
sewing across the centre and
finishing at the tip of one of the
opposite legs.*

2 *Pin the front and back star
pieces together and sew all round
the outside edge, leaving the
marked space open. Now work a
row of stitching 6 mm (¼ in) in
from the cut edge of both sides of
the opening. Clip the turnings at
the base of each leg (see p. 19),
then turn the cushion through to
the right side and stuff lightly.
Ladder stitch across the opening
(see p. 20), using the lines of
stitching as a guide.*

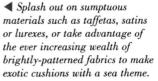

◀ *Splash out on sumptuous
materials such as taffetas, satins
or lurexes, or take advantage of
the ever increasing wealth of
brightly-patterned fabrics to make
exotic cushions with a sea theme.*

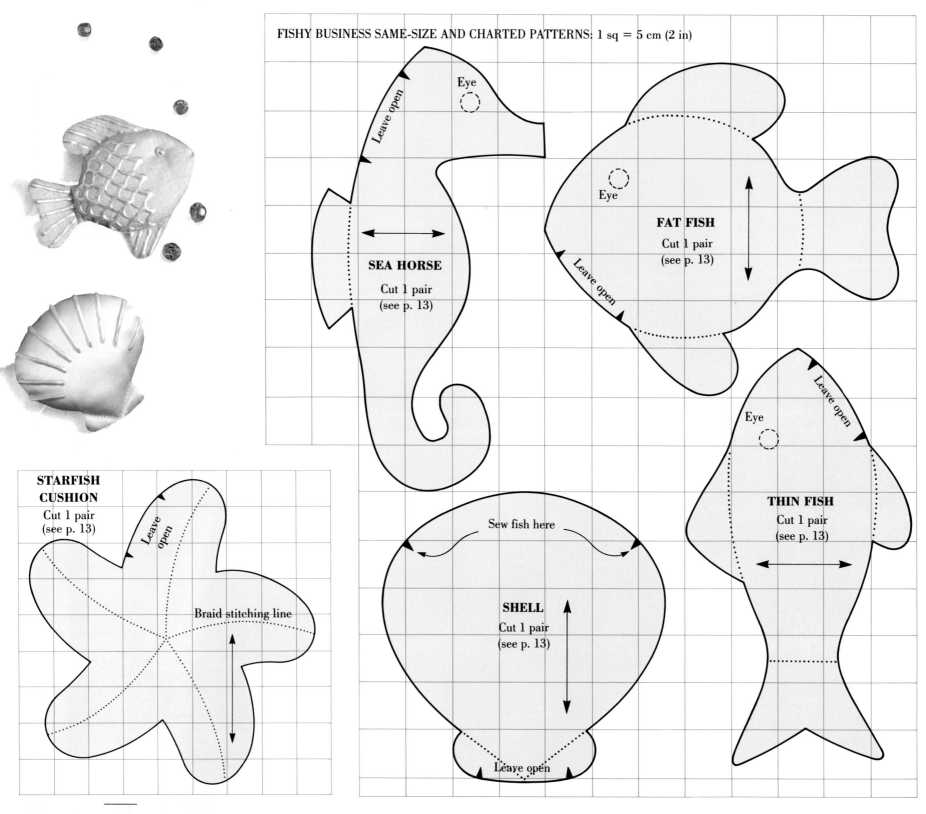

FISHY BUSINESS SAME-SIZE AND CHARTED PATTERNS: 1 sq = 5 cm (2 in)

Leave open

Eye

SEA HORSE

Cut 1 pair
(see p. 13)

Eye

FAT FISH

Cut 1 pair
(see p. 13)

Leave open

Eye

Leave open

THIN FISH

Cut 1 pair
(see p. 13)

**STARFISH
CUSHION**

Cut 1 pair
(see p. 13)

Leave open

Braid stitching line

Sew fish here

SHELL

Cut 1 pair
(see p. 13)

Leave open

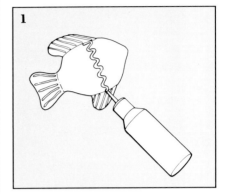

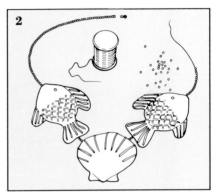

▲ *Pearl fabric paint adds texture and interest to a delicate girl's necklace. Use the range of coloured fabric paints and vibrant materials to create a necklace of brilliant tropical fish.*

MERMAID'S NECKLACE

You Will Need:
Scraps of cream silk and satin
10 cm (1/8 yd) of 90 cm (36 in) wide extra fine iron-on interfacing
Toy stuffing
Clear nylon thread

Approx. 100 small pearl beads and 2 slightly larger beads
Necklace clasp
Pearl outliner fabric paint
Matching sewing thread

Cutting Out:
Trace off the same-size patterns on p. 62 for the fat fish and the shell. Interface a piece of silk to make two fish, and a piece of satin to make one shell.

Take 6 mm (1/4 in) seam turnings throughout.

1 *Make up the fish as for the mobile (pp. 64–65). Make up the shell in the same manner, but this time stitch along the dotted lines after filling with stuffing and joining the opening. Follow the photograph to decorate the shell and fish on one side only with pearl paint, making a pair of fish. Leave the paint to dry completely.*

2 *Using the larger beads, sew an 'eye' on each fish, pulling up the thread to indent the bead. Sew a length of thread to the centre of each fish's tail and thread with three small beads, then sew to the side edges of the shell where marked and tie off securely. Now make a 20 cm (8 in) length of beading starting at each fish's mouth. Knot each end round the two halves of the clasp, and feed the ends of the thread back through the beads to neaten.*

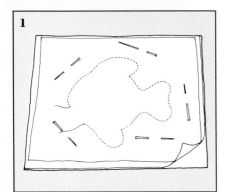

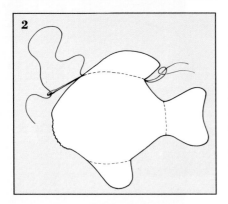

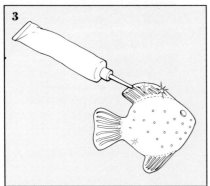

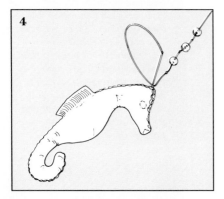

MARINE MOBILE

1 *Fuse the interfacing to the wrong side of the fabric, then cut the fabric in half. Take one fabric half and draw round the pattern on to the interfacing with a pencil, then place the fabric pieces right sides together and sew round the pencil outline, leaving the marked space open.*

2 *Trim away the fabric 3 mm (¹/8 in) from the sewing line and clip the corners (see p. 19). Carefully turn the fish to the right side through the opening, and use a blunt-ended knitting needle to turn out the tail and fins. Following the dotted lines on the pattern, machine stitch through both layers of fabric, then tie off and darn the ends of the thread back into the body.*

3 *Stuff the body lightly, then turn in the raw edges and ladder stitch the opening closed (see p. 20). Following the photograph, decorate one side with glitter paint and leave to set before turning over and decorating the other side to match.*

4 *Make two of each fish and one seahorse. Sew a 90 cm (36 in) length of nylon thread through the top of the seahorse, knot securely and sew the end back into the body. Attach some bead 'bubbles' at random along the thread by first making a double knot, then threading it with a bead, until a 10–15 cm (4–6 in) length has been beaded.*

You Will Need:
Oddments of lurex tissue fabric
in five different colours
20 cm (¹/4 yd) of 90 cm (36 in)
wide extra fine
iron-on interfacing
Toy stuffing
Mobile wires, one 25 cm (10 in)
long and two 15 cm (6 in) long
Clear nylon thread
Approx. 40 iridescent glass beads
A tiny clear plastic ring
Glitter fabric pens in
several colours
Hot glue gun
Matching sewing threads

Cutting Out:
Trace off the same-size patterns on p. 62 for the fat and thin fish and the seahorse. For each creature cut out a piece of interfacing and a matching piece of lurex tissue, roughly twice the size of the pattern piece.

Take 6 mm (¹/4 in) seam turnings throughout.

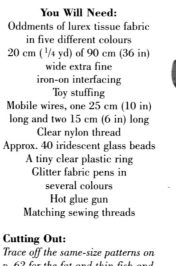

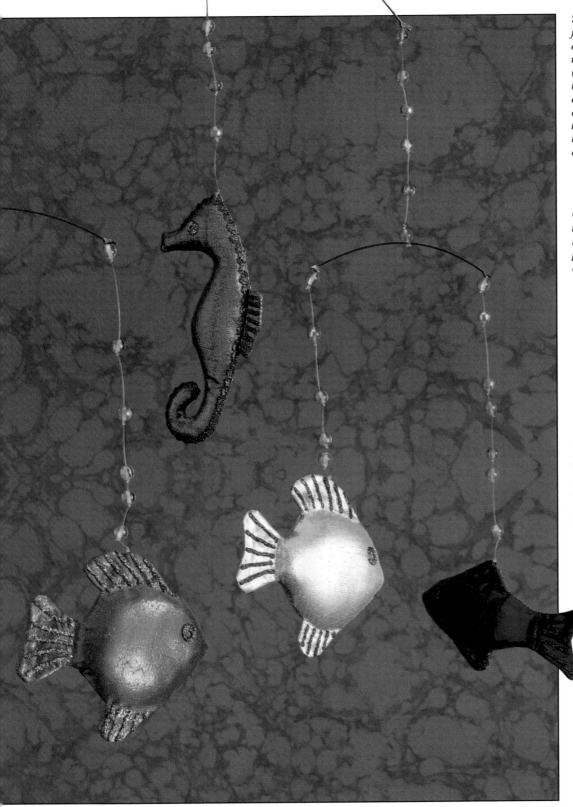

5 *Repeat on the remaining four fish, using 25 cm (10 in) lengths of thread, attaching the thread to the top fin and making 10–15 cm (4–6 in) lengths of beading as before. Tie a fish securely to both ends of the shorter wires, making each knot as close as possible to the last bead. Feed the thread end back through the bead and trim away the excess.*

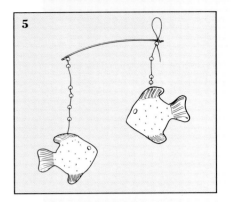

6 *Tie the seahorse thread tightly to the centre of the long wire, making the knot as close as possible to the last bead. Leave the excess thread.*

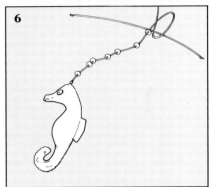

7 *Taking two 25 cm (10 in) lengths of thread, work a 10 cm (4 in) section of beading in the centre of each. Tie one end of each thread to the centre of one of the short wires, then tie the remaining ends to each end of the long wire, neatening the thread ends as in step 5.*

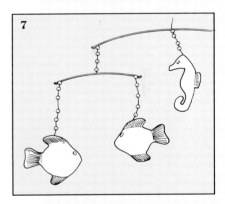

8 *Trim the hanging thread to the required length, then tie it securely to the tiny ring. Hang up the mobile and adjust the position of the threads by sliding them along the wires until the correct balance is attained, then secure the threads in place with tiny spots of glue.*

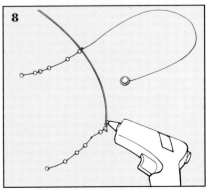

Bugs!

CATERPILLAR

You Will Need:

Oddments of green, yellow and
black jersey panne velvet
Black cotton perlé
embroidery thread
75 g (3 oz) of toy stuffing
Matching sewing threads

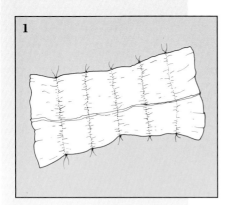

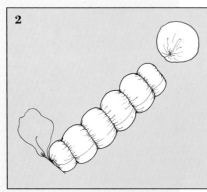

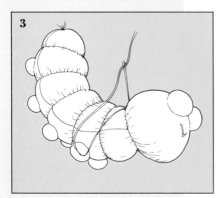

Cutting Out:

*With the pile of the fabric running
parallel to the longer sides, cut a
30 x 13 cm (12 x 5 in) rectangle
of green fabric for the top body
piece and a 30 x 10 cm (12 x 4 in)
rectangle of yellow fabric for the
under body piece. Also cut a
20 cm (8 in) diameter circle of
green fabric for the head, eight
5 cm (2 in) diameter circles of
yellow fabric for the feet,
and two 7 cm (2³/4 in)
diameter circles of
black fabric for the eyes.*

*Take 6 mm (¹/4 in)
seam turnings
throughout.*

1 *Join the top and under
body pieces together along
one long side and press seam
open. Working parallel to the
shorter sides, sew five gathering
threads at 5 cm (2 in) intervals
along the body (see p. 21). Draw
up each thread to measure 15 cm
(6 in), even out the gathers and
tie off the ends of the thread.*

2 *Join the remaining long sides,
then gather round the base edge,
draw up tightly and fasten off.
Turn the body through to the right
side and stuff each section
separately, then gather round the
open top edge, draw up tightly
and fasten off. Make a fabric ball
from the head circle (see p. 16).*

3 *Sew the head to the body, then
embroider the mouth with two
black straight stitches, fastening
off the ends of the thread at eye
positions. Make eyeballs from the
two black circles and sew them in
place. Make fabric balls from the
yellow circles and sew them in
place on the under body to form
feet. Using a double thickness of
thread and a long needle, sew
down the centre of the top body,
starting at the end of the body,
catching each gathering line and
ending at the base of the head.
Draw up the thread to make the
body curve, then fasten off the
thread securely.*

BUTTERFLY

You Will Need:
An oddment of deep pink jersey
panne velvet
20 cm (¼ yd) of 115 cm (45 in)
wide printed figured velvet
A small amount of fine
Terylene wadding
10 g (½ oz) of toy stuffing
10 cm (4 in) of thin black
cord elastic
Two 1 cm (³/₈ in) diameter
black bobbles
Matching sewing threads

1 *Take a pair of wing pieces with right sides together and sandwich them between two matching layers of wadding. Sew all round, leaving the straight edge open. Turn the wing through to the right side, then ladder stitch across the opening (see p. 20). Make all four wings in this manner.*

2 *Join the straight sides of the body, then gather round the narrow base edge, draw up tightly and fasten off. Turn the body through to the right side and stuff firmly, then gather round the open top edge, draw up tightly and fasten off. Make a fabric ball for the head from the panne velvet circle (see p. 16).*

3 *Sew the head securely to the body, then sew the wings to the sides of the body, overlapping the lower wings with the upper wings. Tie a knot in both ends of the elastic and sew a bobble securely to each knot to make the antennae. Fold the elastic in half and sew the fold to the top of the head, then sew through both pieces of the elastic close to the fold to make the antennae stand up.*

Cutting Out:
Trace off the same-size patterns on pp. 70–71 and cut out one butterfly body piece from panne velvet, together with a 10 cm (4 in) diameter circle for the head. Mark the wing sewing lines on the right side of the body piece with chalk. Of each wing pattern cut two pairs from printed velvet, and two pairs from wadding.

Take 6 mm (¼ in) seam turnings throughout.

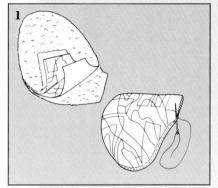

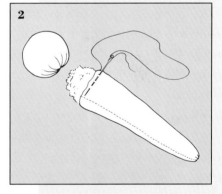

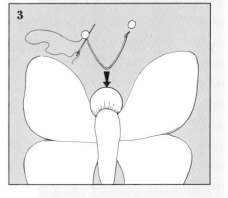

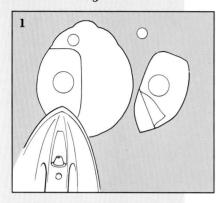

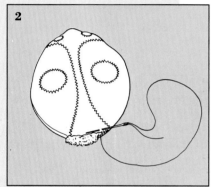

LADYBIRD

You Will Need:
Oddments of black, red and white
jersey panne velvet or
jersey velour
A small amount of iron-on
bonding web
30 g (1¼ oz) of toy stuffing
Matching sewing threads

Cutting Out:
Trace off the same-size patterns on pp. 70–71 and cut out two ladybird body pieces from black fabric. Draw a pair of wing pieces and two 1.5 cm (⁵⁄₈ in) diameter circles for the eye spots on the bonding web backing paper. Fuse the wings to the wrong side of the red fabric, and the spots to the white fabric and cut out.

Take 6 mm (¹⁄₄ in) seam turnings throughout.

1 *Peel off the backing paper from the bonded pieces. Using the dotted lines on the pattern as a guide, position the pieces on one body piece, cover with a cloth and fuse in place with an iron.*

2 *Appliqué the wings and spots by working a small zigzag stitch over the raw edges. With the body pieces placed right sides together, sew all round, leaving the space between the base edges of the wings open. Clip the turnings at the corners (see p. 19), then turn the ladybird to the right side through the opening. Stuff firmly, then ladder stitch across the opening (see p. 20).*

▶ *Lucky Ladybird placemats and coasters are simple to make and bring a splash of colour and fun to any children's tea party.*

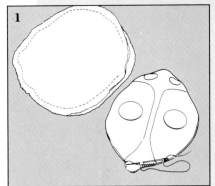

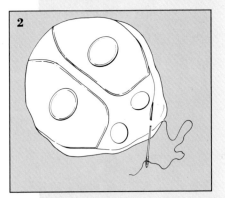

LADYBIRD POT HOLDER

You Will Need:
Oddments of red, black and white
glazed cotton
A small amount of fine
Terylene wadding
A small amount of iron-on
bonding web
Matching sewing threads

Cutting Out:
*Follow the cutting out instructions
for the Ladybird opposite, cutting
out four body pieces from black
fabric as well as four body pieces
from wadding.*

*Take 6 mm (¹/₄ in) seam turnings
throughout.*

1 *Appliqué the wing and eye spots
in place on one body piece as for
the Ladybird (step 2, opposite).
Place the appliquéd piece right
sides together with another body
piece and sandwich them between
two pieces of wadding. Sew all
round the body, leaving the space
between the base edges of the
wings open. Clip turnings at the
corners (see p. 19), turn through
to the right side and ladder stitch
across the opening (see p. 20).
Repeat with the remaining
body pieces.*

2 *Press both ladybirds lightly
with a cool iron then, with the
plain sides facing, join the top
edge of the two bodies together
with ladder stitch, following the
seam lines and working between
the top edges of the two wings.*

LADYBIRD PLACEMATS OR COASTERS

You Will Need
For Each Placemat or Coaster:
Oddments of black, red and white
cotton-backed PVC
A 30 cm (12 in) square of black
felt for the placemat, or a 15 cm
(6 in) square for the coaster
Spray adhesive
Pinking shears
Matching sewing threads

Cutting Out:
*Use the same-size patterns on
pp. 70–71 for the coaster, or
enlarge the patterns to 200%
(either by photocopier or by
charting on to graph paper – see
p. 12) for the placemat. Cut out
one body piece in black and a
pair of wing pieces in red PVC.
Also cut out two white eye spots,
1.5 cm (⁵/₈ in) diameter for the
coaster or 3cm (1¹/₄ in) diameter
for the placemat.*

*Take 6 mm (¹/₄ in) seam turnings
throughout.*

1 *Spray adhesive on to the back
of the wing pieces and eye spots
and, using the dotted lines on the
pattern as a guide, attach them to
the body piece. Appliqué them in
place, using a straight stitch
worked close to the cut edge.
Leave the outside edge of the
wings unsewn.*

2 *Spray adhesive over the back of
the body piece and attach it
diagonally on to the felt square.
Sew in place, stitching close to the
cut edge as before and changing
thread colours to match. Take the
ends of the thread through to the
back, tie them off and darn into
the felt. Trim away the excess felt
close to the edge of the body using
pinking shears (see p. 19).*

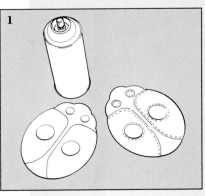

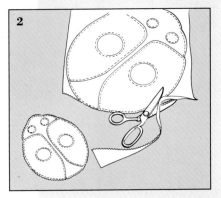

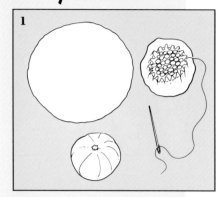

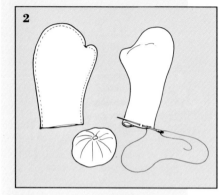

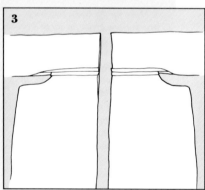

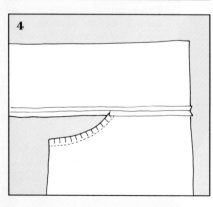

TUMBLING CLOWN

You Will Need:

40 cm (¹/₂ yd) of 115 cm (45 in) wide satin in each of two colours
A 20 cm (8 in) square of felt
30 cm (¹/₃ yd) of 137 cm (54 in) wide nylon net
An oddment of white cotton jersey
Scraps of black and white cotton poplin, red cotton jersey, cotton muslin and black fur fabric
Two 5 cm (2 in) diameter pompoms (see p. 99, step 4)
Lengths of black and red cotton knitting yarn
Red pencil
80 g (3 oz) of dried split peas
150 g (6 oz) of toy stuffing
Clear adhesive
Matching sewing threads

1 Cut four 10 cm (4 in) diameter circles of muslin for the beanbags. Gather round the edge of each circle and draw up tightly (see p. 20), filling each one with 20 g (³/₄ oz) of split peas. Fasten off securely.

2 Sew the hand pieces together in pairs, leaving the top edges open. Trim the seams and clip the turning at the base of the thumb (see p. 19), then turn the hands through to the right side. Stuff them firmly, inserting a beanbag into the centre of the stuffing. Gather round the top edge of the hand, draw up tightly and fasten off. Make both feet in the same manner.

3 Sew the front and back waist edges of one trouser leg to the waist edge on both sides of the differently coloured sleeve/body piece, and press the seam open. Repeat with the other two pieces.

4 Now sew the underarm seam on each sleeve, and the curved outside seam on both trouser pieces. Press the underarm seam open and clip the turnings round the curved trouser seams (see p. 18).

Cutting Out:

Draw out the measurements-only pattern pieces on pp. 78–79 on to plain paper, the charted pieces on p. 76 on to graph paper (see p. 12), and cut out. Cut one trouser leg and one sleeve/body piece from each colour of satin. Cut the remaining pieces from the fabrics stated on the patterns.

Take 6 mm (¹/₄ in) seam turnings throughout.

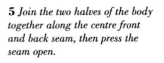

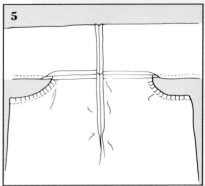

5 *Join the two halves of the body together along the centre front and back seam, then press the seam open.*

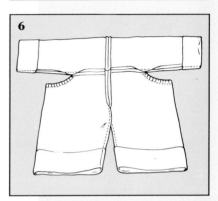

5

6 *Now sew the inside leg seam on each trouser leg and press open. Turn under 5 cm (2 in) around both sleeve hems and both trouser hems and press down.*

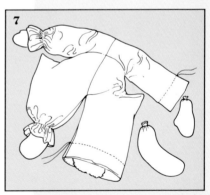

6

7 *Turn the body to the right side through one of the trouser hems. Work a row of machine gathering stitches 4 cm (1¹/₂ in) from the folded edge on each sleeve and trouser hem (see p. 21). Stuff the centre of the body lightly, then stuff the arms and legs very lightly. Draw up the gathering threads to fit round the hands and feet. Pin, then sew in place by hand, working over the machine stitching.*

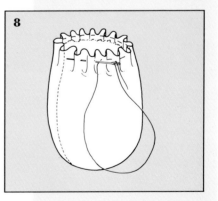

7

8 *Join the side seam of the jersey head rectangle, then work a row of gathering stitches round the base edge, draw up tightly and fasten off. Turn through to the right side and stuff firmly so that the head measures 27 cm (10¹/₂ in) all round. Gather round the top edge, draw it up tightly and fasten off.*

8

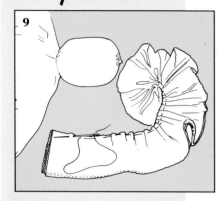

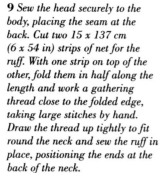

9 Sew the head securely to the body, placing the seam at the back. Cut two 15 x 137 cm (6 x 54 in) strips of net for the ruff. With one strip on top of the other, fold them in half along the length and work a gathering thread close to the folded edge, taking large stitches by hand. Draw the thread up tightly to fit round the neck and sew the ruff in place, positioning the ends at the back of the neck.

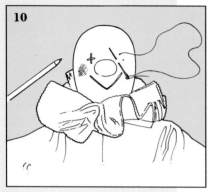

10 Cut a 5 cm (2 in) diameter circle of red jersey for the nose and make an oval fabric ball (see p. 16). Sew the nose to the face, placing it horizontally 5 cm (2 in) up from the neck edge. Mark the positions of the eyes and mouth with pins, then embroider them with straight stitches, using the cotton yarn and a long needle and fastening off the ends of the yarn at the top of the head. Blush the cheeks by rubbing gently with the pencil.

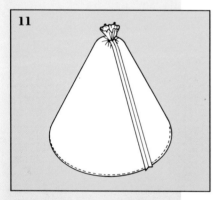

11 Join the hat side seam, then trim the seam (see p. 19). Work a row of machine stitching close to the base edge to prevent it stretching, then gather round the top edge, draw up tightly and fasten off.

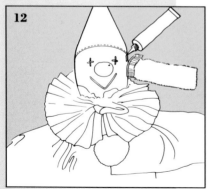

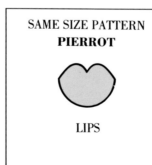

12 Turn the hat through to the right side and stuff lightly. Position and pin on the clown's head, then sew in place, working backstitch over the line of machine stitching. Cut a 3 x 15 cm (1¼ x 6 in) strip of fur fabric, having the shorter side running parallel to the fabric selvedge, for the hair. Glue the hair in place in line with the base of the hat. Sew the pompoms to the centre front seam 5 cm (2 in) each side of the waist seam. Separate the layers of the net on the ruff to fluff it out.

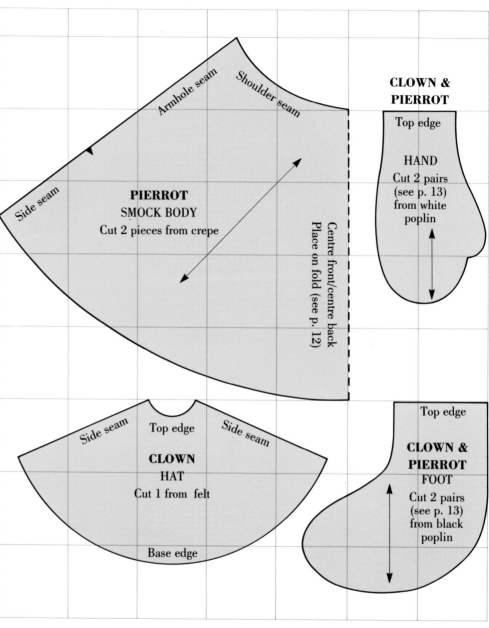

CLOWN & PIERROT

Top edge

HAND
Cut 2 pairs
(see p. 13)
from white
poplin

PIERROT
SMOCK BODY
Cut 2 pieces from crepe

Armhole seam • Shoulder seam

Side seam

Centre front/centre back
Place on fold (see p. 12)

Side seam • Top edge • Side seam

CLOWN
HAT
Cut 1 from felt

Base edge

Top edge

CLOWN & PIERROT
FOOT
Cut 2 pairs
(see p. 13)
from black
poplin

SAME SIZE PATTERN
PIERROT

LIPS

TUMBLING CLOWNS AND PIERROT
CHARTED PATTERN PIECES: 1 sq = 5 cm (2 in)

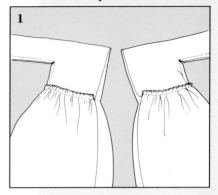

PIERROT

You Will Need:

80 cm (⁷/₈ yd) of 115 cm (45 in) wide cream polyester crêpe

60 cm (²/₃ yd) of 137 cm (54 in) wide cream nylon bridal tulle

An oddment of white cotton jersey

A small amount of black jersey panne velvet and white cotton poplin

Scraps of black cotton poplin, cotton muslin, and black and pink felt

1.40 m (1¹/₂ yd) of 12 mm (¹/₂ in) wide black satin ribbon

20 cm (8 in) of 12 mm (¹/₂ in) wide white cotton straight tape

Two 5 cm (2 in) diameter black pompoms (see step p. 99, step 4)

A length of deep pink cotton knitting yarn

Pink pencil

75 g (3 oz) of dried split peas

150 g (6 oz) of toy stuffing

Clear adhesive

Matching sewing threads

Cutting Out:

Draw out the measurements-only pattern pieces on pp. 78–79 on to plain paper, and the charted pieces opposite on to graph paper (see p. 12), and cut out. Cut out two trouser pieces from crêpe. Cut out the remaining pieces from the fabrics stated on the patterns. Tack down the centre front line on one smock body piece.

Take 6 mm (¹/₄ in) seam turnings throughout.

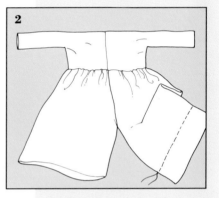

1 *Fold each poplin body piece in half and join the side and arm seams, then clip the seam turning at the underarm (see p. 18). Gather the waist edge of each trouser piece, draw up to fit the body waist, then sew together with the body pieces along the waist seam.*

2 *Join the two halves of the body together and sew the inside leg seams as for the clown (steps 5–6, p. 75). Turn the body through to the right side, turn up the trouser hems and work gathering threads as before.*

◄ *A stock comic character from French pantomime, the Pierrot has been transformed here into an exquisite doll that could easily become a family heirloom.*

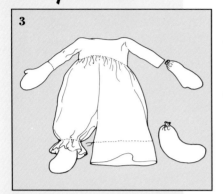

3 *Stuff the body, arms and legs as for the clown (step 7, p. 75). Make up weighted hands and feet as before (step 2, p. 74), draw up the gathered trouser hems and sew the feet in place. Turn under 6 mm (¹/₄ in) at the base of each arm, insert the hands into the openings and handsew in place.*

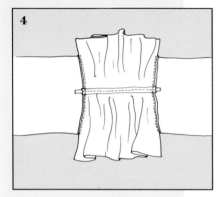

4 *Sew the smock front and back pieces together at the shoulder seam, then sew the centre of the straight tape to the seam, following the previous stitching line, to prevent the seam stretching. Now sew the sleeve heads to the armholes.*

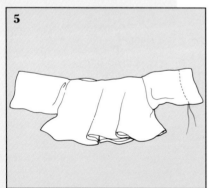

5 *Join the smock side and sleeve seams. Turn under 6 mm (¹/₄ in), then 6 mm (¹/₄ in) again round the main hem and sew down. Turn under a hem and work a gathering thread on each sleeve as for the clown. Turn the smock through to the right side.*

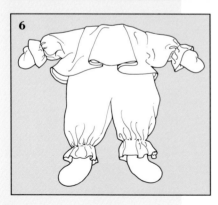

6 *Fit the smock on the doll, then catch the smock to the body at the neck point with a few stitches. Draw up the gathering threads round the sleeve hems and sew to the hands as before (step 7, p. 75).*

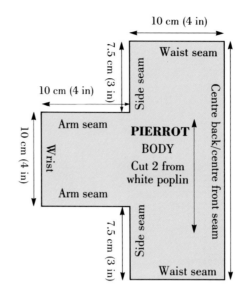

10 cm (4 in)

7.5 cm (3 in)

Waist seam

Side seam

10 cm (4 in)

Arm seam

10 cm (4 in)

Wrist

Arm seam

PIERROT
BODY
Cut 2 from white poplin

Centre back/centre front seam

7.5 cm (3 in)

Side seam

Waist seam

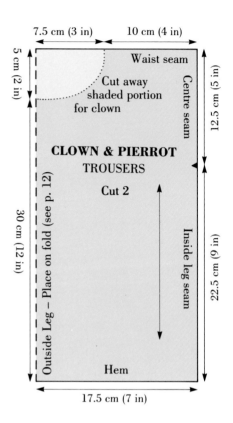

7.5 cm (3 in)

10 cm (4 in)

5 cm (2 in)

Waist seam

Cut away shaded portion for clown

Centre seam

12.5 cm (5 in)

CLOWN & PIERROT
TROUSERS
Cut 2

30 cm (12 in)

Outside Leg – Place on fold (see p. 12)

Inside leg seam

22.5 cm (9 in)

Hem

17.5 cm (7 in)

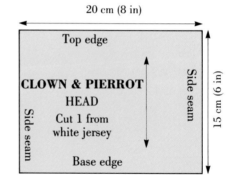

20 cm (8 in)

Top edge

Side seam

CLOWN & PIERROT
HEAD
Cut 1 from white jersey

Side seam

15 cm (6 in)

Base edge

TUMBLING CLOWNS AND PIERROT
MEASUREMENTS-ONLY PATTERNS

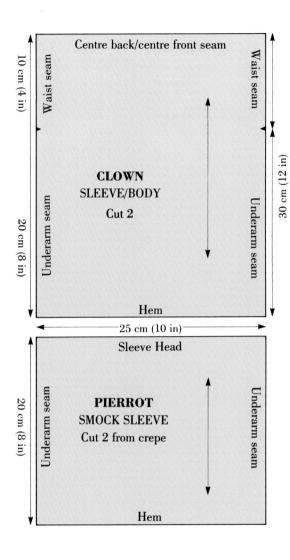

Centre back/centre front seam

Waist seam

10 cm (4 in)

Waist seam

30 cm (12 in)

CLOWN
SLEEVE/BODY
Cut 2

Underarm seam

20 cm (8 in)

Underarm seam

Hem

25 cm (10 in)

Sleeve Head

Underarm seam

20 cm (8 in)

PIERROT
SMOCK SLEEVE
Cut 2 from crepe

Underarm seam

Hem

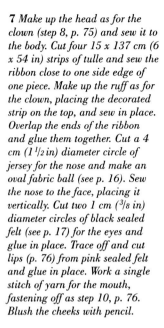

◄ *These measurements-only patterns are drawn to scale. They can be drawn directly on to card following the measurements given.*

▼ *There is nothing sad about these clowns as they perform their acrobatics across the page. A collection of colourful, lively clowns such as these will make everybody smile.*

7 Make up the head as for the clown (step 8, p. 75) and sew it to the body. Cut four 15 x 137 cm (6 x 54 in) strips of tulle and sew the ribbon close to one side edge of one piece. Make up the ruff as for the clown, placing the decorated strip on the top, and sew in place. Overlap the ends of the ribbon and glue them together. Cut a 4 cm (1½ in) diameter circle of jersey for the nose and make an oval fabric ball (see p. 16). Sew the nose to the face, placing it vertically. Cut two 1 cm (³/₈ in) diameter circles of black sealed felt (see p. 17) for the eyes and glue in place. Trace off and cut lips (p. 76) from pink sealed felt and glue in place. Work a single stitch of yarn for the mouth, fastening off as step 10, p. 76. Blush the cheeks with pencil.

8 Cut a 30 cm (12 in) diameter semicircle from panne velvet for the headscarf, placing the straight edge parallel to the selvedge. Turn under 6 mm (¼ in) along the straight edge and machine stitch close to the fold. Pin it to the head, positioning the point where the ends meet at the left side of the head. Sew the scarf in place, working backstitch over the line of machine stitching.

9 Pleat the curved edge to fit and sew the pleats in place at the side of the head. Cut a 10 cm (4 in) square of velvet and fold diagonally. Sew 5 cm (2 in) along each side seam, starting at the folded end. Turn the piece through to the right side, trim away the excess fabric, leaving 6 mm (¼ in) to tuck inside, and oversew the opening.

10 Tie a tight knot in the centre of the piece and sew it to the headscarf. Position and sew the pompoms to the centre front of the smock, then remove tacking thread. Separate the layers of tulle to fluff them out.

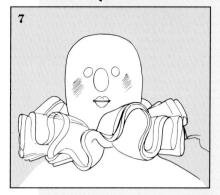

7

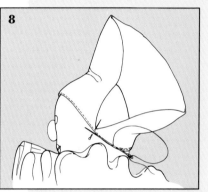

8

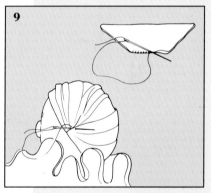

9

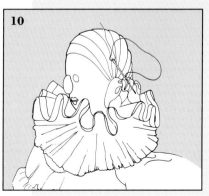

10

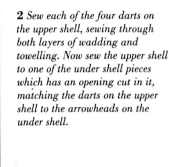

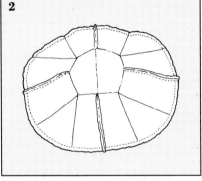

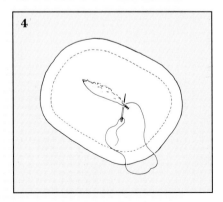

TERRY TURTLE

1 *Using the pen, transfer the quilting lines on to the right side of the towelling upper shell piece. Pin on top of the matching piece of wadding and quilt by sewing over the marked lines with a straight stitch.*

2 *Sew each of the four darts on the upper shell, sewing through both layers of wadding and towelling. Now sew the upper shell to one of the under shell pieces which has an opening cut in it, matching the darts on the upper shell to the arrowheads on the under shell.*

3 *Turn to the right side through the opening. With the quilted side of the shell uppermost, topstitch all round 2.5 cm (1 in) in from the edge. Fill with chippings, then oversew edges of opening together. You will probably find that scraps of chippings cling to the outside of the shell. To remove them, wrap some parcel tape round your hand, sticky side out, and use to pat the fabric.*

4 *Take the remaining under shell pieces together, having the piece with the opening cut in it uppermost. Pin on top of the matching wadding piece and sew all round. Turn to right side through opening, then topstitch 2.5 cm (1 in) in from the edge and oversew opening as before.*

You Will Need:
40 cm (¹/₂ yd) of 90 cm (36 in) wide jade green towelling
30 cm (¹/₃ yd) of 90 cm (36 in) wide yellow towelling
Scraps of black and white cotton-backed PVC and turquoise towelling
An oddment of thick Terylene wadding
100 g (4 oz) of foam chippings
Pink soft embroidery cotton thread
Air-vanishing embroiderer's marking pen
Clear adhesive
Matching sewing threads

Cutting Out:
Enlarge the patterns on p. 82 to 200% (either by photocopier or by charting on to graph paper – see p. 12), making the top body pattern by trimming off the head portion of the under body pattern along the dotted neck line. Add 6 mm (¹/₄ in) seam turnings to each piece. Cut upper and under shell pieces from jade towelling, cutting the central opening in two of the under shell pieces only. Also cut one upper shell piece and one under shell piece from wadding. Cut top and under body pieces and head pieces from yellow towelling, cutting the opening in the top body piece only. Also cut two 4 cm (1¹/₂ in) diameter circles of turquoise towelling for the eyeballs, one 2 cm (³/₄ in) diameter circle of white PVC for the eyes, and two 1 cm (³/₈ in) diameter circles of black PVC for the pupils.

Take 6 mm (¹/₄ in) seam turnings throughout.

▶ *Ordinary towelling and household sponge are used to create these delightful bathtime companions. Make plenty of terrapins to give as gifts to young relatives and friends– but make sure you keep some for yourself!*

5 *Mark the positions of the eyes and mouth on the right side of the fabric with the pen, then join the head pieces together along the top edge. Now sew the head and top body pieces together along the neck edge, then sew the top and under body pieces together and clip the turnings round the curves (see p. 18).*

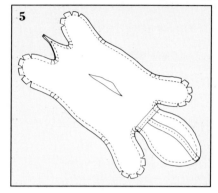

6 *Turn to the right side through the opening, then stuff the head, legs and tail with the foam chippings, keeping the centre of the body unstuffed. Pin the two layers of fabric together to keep the chippings in place, then oversew the edges of the opening together. Sew securely to the underside of the upper shell with backstitch, following the line of the pins.*

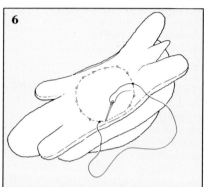

7 *Place the under shell and the body together, having the opening on the under shell next to the body, then sew the sides of the shells together by hand, sewing between the two quilted lines either side of the side dart on the upper shell.*

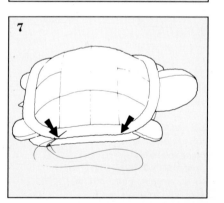

8 *Fastening the ends of the thread at one eye position, embroider the mouth with soft cotton, working one stitch between the two mouth points and catching down in the centre to form a smile with a single small stitch. Cut the white PVC circle in half and glue to the towelling circles, placing the straight edge in the centre of the circle. Sew all round, close to the edge, then glue the black circles in place and sew down as before. Make the towelling circles into fabric balls (see p. 16), stuffing them with foam chippings. Sew them securely to the eye positions.*

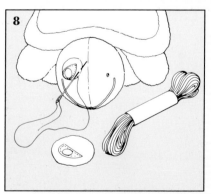

TEENY TINY TURTLES

You Will Need:
Coloured household
sponge cloths
6 mm (¹/4 in) diameter glue-on
joggle eyes
Hot glue gun and clear adhesive

Cutting Out:
Reduce the under body and under shell pattern pieces opposite on . p. 82 to 50% (either by photocopier or by charting on to graph paper – see p. 12), then make an additional inner shell pattern by trimming off 6 mm (¹/4 in) from the under shell pattern. Cut two under shell pieces and one inner shell piece, together with a 3.5 x 2.5 cm (1³/8 x 1 in) rectangular shell pad, from one coloured cloth, then one body piece from a contrasting coloured cloth.

Take 6 mm (¹/4 in) seam turnings throughout.

1 *Using clear adhesive, glue the eyes to the head. Leave to set until hard. Glue the shell pad to the back of the inner shell piece with the glue gun. Glue the padded inner shell to the top of one under shell piece, then glue the body to the underneath of this shell. Glue the remaining under shell in place along the side edges between the front and back legs, holding the shells together tightly until the glue has cooled and set.*

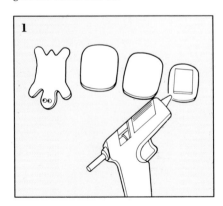

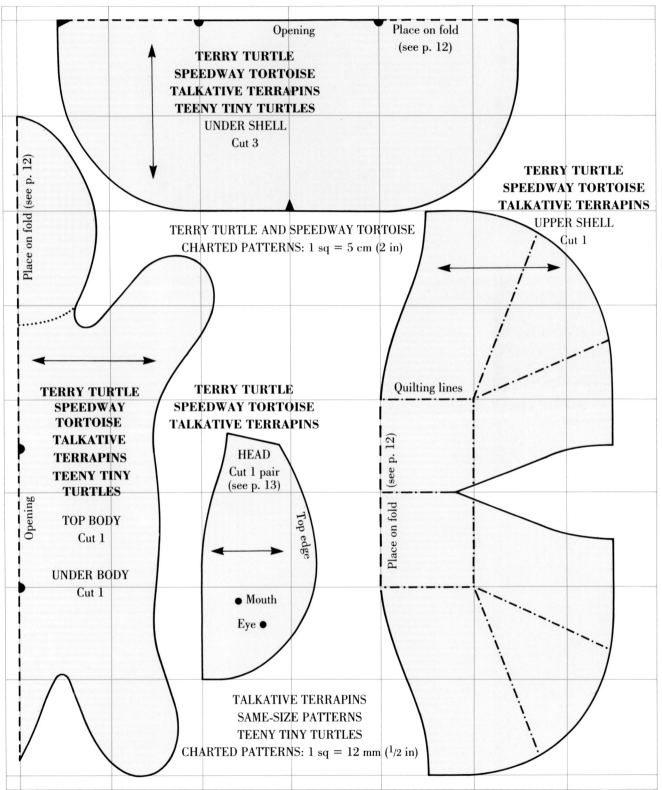

**TERRY TURTLE
SPEEDWAY TORTOISE
TALKATIVE TERRAPINS
TEENY TINY TURTLES**
UNDER SHELL
Cut 3

Opening

Place on fold
(see p. 12)

Place on fold (see p. 12)

TERRY TURTLE AND SPEEDWAY TORTOISE
CHARTED PATTERNS: 1 sq = 5 cm (2 in)

**TERRY TURTLE
SPEEDWAY TORTOISE
TALKATIVE TERRAPINS**
UPPER SHELL
Cut 1

**TERRY TURTLE
SPEEDWAY
TORTOISE
TALKATIVE
TERRAPINS
TEENY TINY
TURTLES**

TOP BODY
Cut 1

UNDER BODY
Cut 1

Opening

**TERRY TURTLE
SPEEDWAY TORTOISE
TALKATIVE TERRAPINS**

HEAD
Cut 1 pair
(see p. 13)

Top edge

● Mouth

Eye ●

Quilting lines

Place on fold (see p. 12)

TALKATIVE TERRAPINS
SAME-SIZE PATTERNS
TEENY TINY TURTLES
CHARTED PATTERNS: 1 sq = 12 mm (¹/2 in)

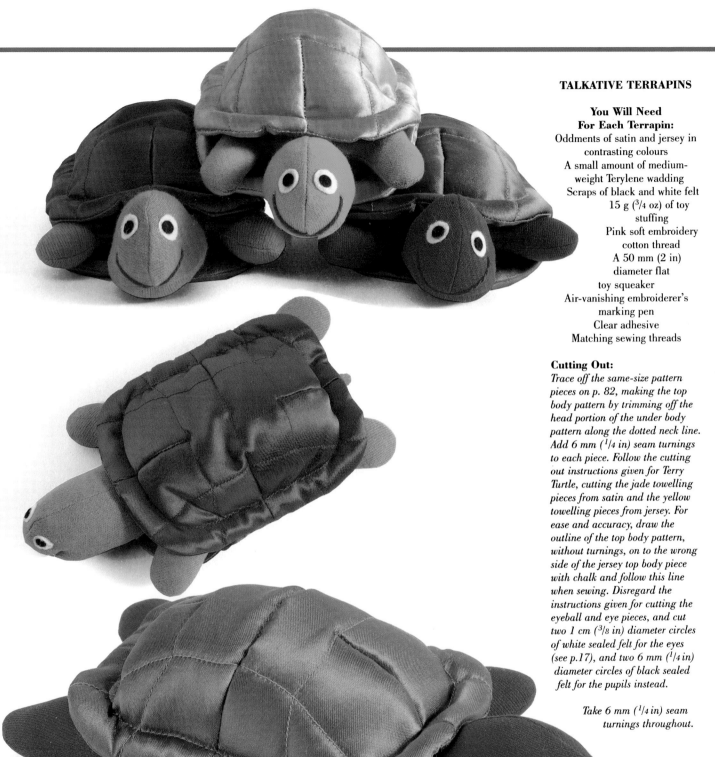

TALKATIVE TERRAPINS

You Will Need
For Each Terrapin:

Oddments of satin and jersey in
contrasting colours
A small amount of medium-
weight Terylene wadding
Scraps of black and white felt
15 g (³/4 oz) of toy
stuffing
Pink soft embroidery
cotton thread
A 50 mm (2 in)
diameter flat
toy squeaker
Air-vanishing embroiderer's
marking pen
Clear adhesive
Matching sewing threads

Cutting Out:

*Trace off the same-size pattern
pieces on p. 82, making the top
body pattern by trimming off the
head portion of the under body
pattern along the dotted neck line.
Add 6 mm (¹/4 in) seam turnings
to each piece. Follow the cutting
out instructions given for Terry
Turtle, cutting the jade towelling
pieces from satin and the yellow
towelling pieces from jersey. For
ease and accuracy, draw the
outline of the top body pattern,
without turnings, on to the wrong
side of the jersey top body piece
with chalk and follow this line
when sewing. Disregard the
instructions given for cutting the
eyeball and eye pieces, and cut
two 1 cm (³/8 in) diameter circles
of white sealed felt for the eyes
(see p.17), and two 6 mm (¹/4 in)
diameter circles of black sealed
felt for the pupils instead.*

*Take 6 mm (¹/4 in) seam
turnings throughout.*

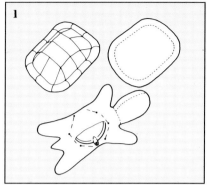

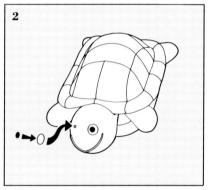

1 *Following the instructions given
for the turtle, make up the upper
and under shells (steps 1–4,
p. 80), topstitching 12 mm (¹/2 in)
in from the outside edge. Also
make up, stuff and pin the body,
leaving the opening unsewn
(step 5, p. 81). Slip the squeaker
into the body, then oversew the
edges of the opening together.*

2 *Assemble the shells and body,
then embroider the mouth,
following the instructions given
for the turtle (see steps 6–8,
p. 81). Glue the white felt circles
in place at the eye positions, then
add the black felt pupils, using a
pair of tweezers to hold the circles
while gluing and fixing in place.*

SPEEDWAY TORTOISE

You Will Need
For the Tortoise :
40 cm (¹/₂ yd) of 115 cm (45 in)
wide royal blue jersey satin
30 cm (¹/₃ yd) of 150 cm (60 in)
wide turquoise tracksuit jersey
A scrap of pink jersey
An oddment of thick
Terylene wadding
Pair of 22 mm (⁷/₈ in) diameter
domed safety toy eyes
100 g (4 oz) of toy stuffing
Pink soft embroidery
cotton thread
Air-vanishing embroiderer's
marking pen
Clear adhesive
Matching sewing threads

You Will Need
For the Trolley :
A 20 cm (8 in) diameter round
plywood plaque
42 cm (16¹/₂ in) of 8 mm (⁵/₁₆ in)
square wood strip
Four 6 cm (2¹/₂ in) diameter
wooden toy wheels
Four 30 mm (1¹/₄ in) dome-
headed wood screws to fit wheels
A screw eye
Pink and yellow tinted
wood varnishes
1.20 m (1¹/₄ yd) of thin
yellow cord
A large yellow wooden bead
10 cm (4 in) of blue Velcro
Wood glue and contact adhesive
Wood saw, bradawl, screwdriver,
and paintbrush

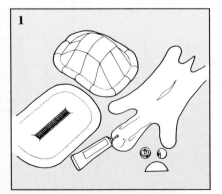

Cutting Out:
Enlarge the patterns on p. 82 to 200% (either by photocopier or by charting on to graph paper – see p. 12) and follow the cutting out instructions given for Terry Turtle (p. 80). Cut the jade towelling pieces from blue jersey, and the yellow towelling pieces from turquoise jersey. Disregard the instructions given for cutting the eyeball and eye pieces, and cut two 5 cm (2 in) diameter circles of pink jersey for the eyelids instead.

Take 6 mm (¹/₄ in) seam turnings throughout.

▶ *Not such a slow coach, our speedway tortoise may well have found a way to overtake the hare! His trolley is made from ordinary plywood and requires no special skills to put together.*

1 *Make up upper and under shells as for the turtle (steps 1–4, p. 80). If making the trolley, sew the hooked section of the Velcro centrally to completed under shell. Make up the body as for the turtle, but leave unstuffed. To prevent the fabric from laddering, dab a spot of clear adhesive at the eye positions and leave to set hard before making holes to fit the eye shafts. Fold the eyelid circles in half and glue the curved edges together. Glue eyelids to the toy eyes, stretching to remove puckers, taking excess fabric to back of the eyes and gluing in place.*

2 *Fix the eyes to the head, then stuff the body and assemble with the shells as for the turtle. Using a long needle, work the mouth with soft cotton as for the turtle, but fasten off the ends of the thread in the centre of the neck seam, then darn the ends back into the body. Sew the back of the neck and the lip of the shell to the front dart of the shell with a few stitches to make the head face upwards.*

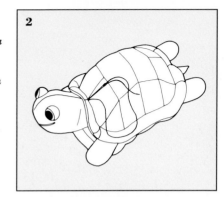

3 *To make the trolley, cut the wood strip in half to make two 21 cm (8^1/$_4$ in) lengths, and glue to the back of the plaque with wood glue, placing each one 4 cm (1^1/$_2$ in) in from the edge of the plaque, making sure that the strips extend equally outside the edge of the circle. Leave to set.*

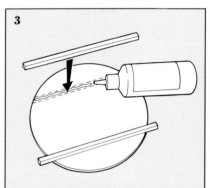

4 *Paint the trolley and wheels with three coats of varnish, leaving to dry thoroughly between coats. Make a hole in the end of each strip of wood with the bradawl, then screw the wheels in place, making sure they turn freely. Also make a hole in the middle of the front strip of wood and screw in the screw eye.*

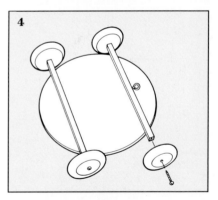

5 *Position and glue the remaining looped section of Velcro down the centre of the trolley, using contact adhesive. Tie a knot at one end of the cord, then thread the bead up to the knot and push the raw end of the cord into the bead to neaten. Tie another knot at the base of the bead, then thread the opposite end of the cord through the screw eye. Make a knot in the end, trim the cord to neaten and seal with a dab of wood glue. Attach the tortoise to the trolley.*

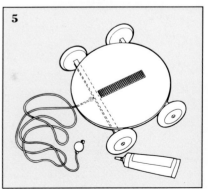

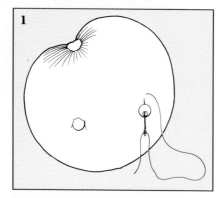

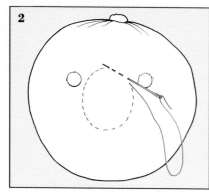

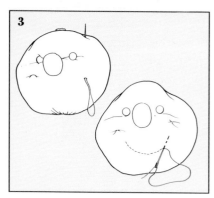

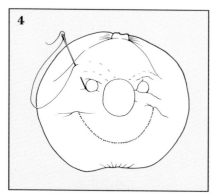

THE BASIC FEATURES

1 *Fasten a long length of thread in the centre of the back seam, take the needle through the head and draw out at one of the eye positions. Thread the needle through a bead or toy eye, insert the needle close to where you drew it out and return it to the back seam. Draw up the thread tightly to embed the eye and fasten off securely. Repeat for the other eye. If you are using joggle eyes, omit the bead or toy eye and take a stitch to indent each eye socket, then glue the eyes in place.*

2 *For the nose, draw out the needle at the nose position on the front of the face and fasten off the thread with a French knot. Work a circle, or oval, of running stitches, then draw up to form a nose and fasten off as before.*

3 *To shape the cheeks and mouth, insert the needle close to the French knot, draw out at a point below one eye and fasten off with a French knot. Insert the needle at this point and draw out above the eye. Take a stitch, then return and draw out the needle at the lower point. Draw up tightly to shape cheek and fasten off with another French knot. Repeat on the other side of the face. Work a curved row of running stitches between the two lower cheek points, draw up to shape the mouth and fasten off.*

4 *To form the eyebrows, insert the needle at the side of the mouth and draw it out at the end of one eyebrow. Work the first eyebrow with ladder stitch (see p. 20), passing the needle under the fabric and working towards the nose. Pass the needle under the nose and work the second eyebrow from nose to outer end. Draw up the thread to shape, fasten off with a French knot and return the needle to the back seam. Use this method to make a narrow nose instead of a round one if desired.*

You Will Need:
Soft sculpture needles or
long darners
Buttonhole thread to match fabric
Black wooden or plastic beads,
sew-on toy eyes or glue-on
joggle eyes
Hot glue gun (to attach
joggle eyes)

To practise the technique, make up a simple head from a rectangle of jersey. Machine stitch the short sides, then work gathering stitches round the base edge, draw up and fasten off. Turn the head to the right side, stuff firmly, then gather and fasten off the top edge as before. Position the seam at the back of the head.

Where jersey pattern pieces are given in the form of measurements, 'long' means parallel to the fabric's selvedge, and 'wide' means across the fabric at right angles to the selvedge. Cut in this way, the 'wide' side of the piece will have more stretch than the 'long' side.

Take 6 mm (¹/4 in) seam turnings throughout.

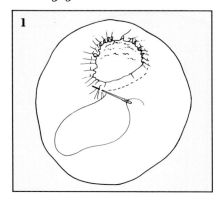

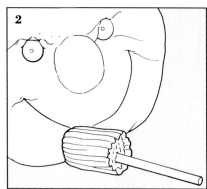

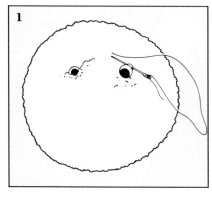

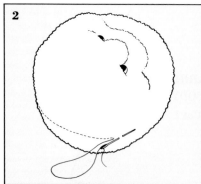

PUMPKINS

You Will Need:
Burnt orange jersey fabric
Beige jumbo corduroy
2 cm (^{3}/$_4$ in) black wooden beads
Toy stuffing
Matching sewing and
buttonhole threads

1 *Join the short edges, then work
gathering stitches round one end,
draw the thread up tightly and
fasten off. Turn the pumpkin
through to the right side and stuff
firmly. Gather round the top edge,
draw it up tightly and fasten off.*

2 *Work the basic features
following steps 1–4 on p. 86. Join
the side seam of the stalk, gather
round the top edge, draw up
tightly and fasten off. Turn
through to the right side, fold
under turning round base edge,
then stuff firmly. Sew the stalk
securely to the top of the pumpkin.*

Cutting Out:
*Cut a rectangle or square of jersey
measuring between 40–60 cm
(16–24 in) wide and 20–40 cm
(8–16 in) long. Vary the sizes to
make different shaped
pumpkins. Also cut a
12 cm (4^3/$_4$ in)
wide x 8 cm
(3^1/$_8$ in) long
piece of
corduroy
for the
stem.*

CAULIFLOWER

You Will Need:
A 50 cm (19^1/$_2$ in) diameter
circle of cream curly fur fabric
Green cotton poplin and
matching green felt
Pair of 2 cm (^{3}/$_4$ in) diameter
sew-on toy eyes
Anti-fray fabric sealer
Toy stuffing
Matching sewing and
buttonhole threads

1 *Using large stitches, gather the
round edge of the fur fabric circle
and draw up tightly, stuffing
firmly, and fasten off. First work
the nose (p. 86), then sew the eyes
securely in place.*

2 *Now work the remaining
features. Sew a gathering thread
round the side of the cauliflower,
draw up slightly to form a drum
shape and fasten off.*

Cutting Out:
*Use the patterns on
pp. 88–89 to cut six
leaves from the poplin
and six stalks from the
felt. Also cut a 12 cm
(4^3/$_4$ in) diameter circle
of felt for the base.*

▼ *Scraps of old towelling, clothing or furnishing fabrics can all be used to create a basketful of pumpkins, aubergines, peas, sweetcorn, carrots, tomatoes and cauliflower – each vegetable with a character of its own.*

You Will Need:
Dark green jersey towelling
Emerald green felt and cotton poplin
Two 1 cm (³/8 in) black wooden beads for eyes
Coarse string
Toy stuffing
Matching sewing and buttonhole threads

Cutting Out:
Cut a 25 cm (10 in) diameter circle of towelling for the head, and a 15 x 12 cm (6 x 4³/4 in) rectangle in both felt and poplin for the stem.

3 *Seal the edges of the leaves with fabric sealer and leave to dry. Sew a felt stalk to the centre of each leaf, leaving the base edge open, and stuff lightly.*

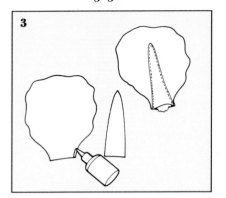

4 *Pin three leaves, evenly spaced, round the cauliflower and catchstitch them in place across the base edge of each leaf. Now sew the remaining leaves in between the previous ones. Catch the top of each stalk to the side of the cauliflower with a few stitches.*

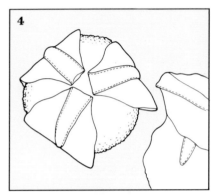

5 *Work gathering stitches round the edge of the felt circle and draw the thread up tightly, padding the circle lightly to form a flat cushion. Fasten off, then sew to the base of the cauliflower.*

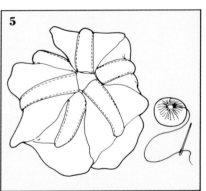

BROCCOLI

1 *Make up the head as for the cauliflower opposite, stuffing it lightly to form a cushion shape. Pin the felt and poplin stem pieces together and sew a row of stitching 5 cm (2 in) in from, and parallel to, both short sides. Fold the stem piece in half with the poplin on the outside and stitch the side seam, then gather round the base, draw up tightly and fasten off. Turn the stem through to the right side and stuff each of the three channels firmly. Sew the top edge of the stem securely to the back of the head, then wrap string twice round the stem and tie in a bow.*

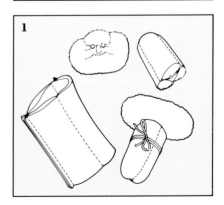

91

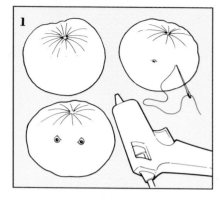

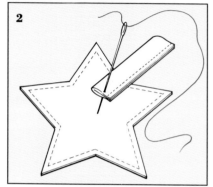

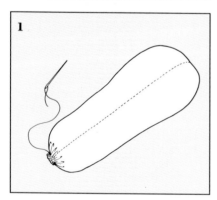

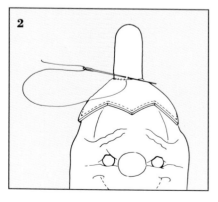

TOMATOES

You Will Need:
Red lustre jersey
Deep green felt
6 mm (¹/₄ in) diameter
glue-on joggle eyes
Toy stuffing
Matching sewing and
buttonhole threads
Clear adhesive and hot glue gun

Cutting Out:
*Cut a 25 cm (10 in) diameter
circle of jersey. Cut a 1 x 2.5 cm
(³/₈ x 1 in) strip of felt for the
stem and a calyx from sealed felt,
using the pattern on p. 88.*

1 *Gather round the edge of the
circle and draw it up tightly,
stuffing firmly and pushing raw
edges inside to neaten. Fasten off,
then mark eye depressions with
two stitches and glue the joggle
eyes securely in place.*

2 *Work the remaining basic
features (p. 86). Sew all round the
calyx, close to the edge, then fold
the stem strip in half and sew
close to the cut edge. Sew stalk to
the top of the calyx, then glue to
the top of the tomato.*

EGGPLANT

1 *Join the body side seam, then
gather round the base, draw the
thread up tightly and fasten off.
Turn through to the right side and
stuff firmly. Gather round the top,
draw the thread up tightly and
fasten off.*

You Will Need:
Wine coloured lycra
Bright green felt
Two 1 cm (³/₈ in) black wooden
beads for eyes
Toy stuffing
Matching sewing and
buttonhole threads

Cutting Out:
*Use the patterns on pp. 88–89
to cut a body piece from lycra
and a calyx from felt. Cut a
6 x 4 cm (2³/₈ x 1¹/₂ in)
piece of felt for the stalk.*

2 *Work the basic features (p. 86).
Sew round the pointed edge of the
calyx, close to the edge, then
hand oversew the side seam.
Gather round the top edge, draw
up tightly and fasten off. Glue the
calyx to the top of the body. Join
the shorter sides of the stalk piece,
then gather round the top edge,
draw up tightly and fasten off.
Turn the stalk to the right side,
stuff firmly, then sew securely to
the top of the calyx.*

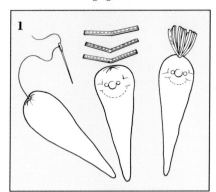

CARROTS

You Will Need:
Orange jersey fabric
Leaf green felt
Two 3 mm (¹/8 in) black plastic
beads for eyes
Toy stuffing
Matching sewing and
buttonhole threads

Cutting Out:
Using the pattern on p. 89 cut out a body piece from jersey. Also cut a 1 x 25 cm (³/8 x 10 in) strip of felt for the leaf stalks.

1 *Join the body side seam to make a cone, then turn through to the right side. Stuff firmly, gather round the top edge and draw up tightly, pushing raw edges inside to neaten. Fasten off, then work the basic features (p. 86). Fold the stalk strip in half and sew close to the cut edge. Cut it into three 7.5 cm (3 in) lengths. Hold the strips together and fold them in half, then sew the fold securely to the top of the carrot to form a bunch of stalks.*

PEAS

You Will Need:
Bright green PVC, jersey fabric
and felt
3 mm (¹/8 in) glue-on joggle eyes
Toy stuffing
Matching sewing and
buttonhole threads
Clear adhesive and hot glue gun

Cutting Out:
Using the patterns on p. 88, for each pod cut out a pair of pod pieces from PVC, and a calyx piece from sealed felt (see p. 17). For the peas, cut three 5 cm (2 in) diameter circles of jersey.

1 *To make a closed pod, join the pod pieces along the back seam, trim the seam and turn to the right side. Pad with a roll of stuffing and glue the front edges together, then sew along the front edge. Glue a calyx to the top of the pod, folding the stem in half and gluing together.*

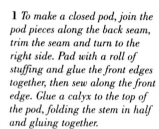

2 *To make an open pod, join the back pod seam as before, trim and turn the pod to the right side. Make three fabric balls from the jersey circles (see p. 16) and work a mouth on each with running stitches. Glue the eyes securely in place, then glue the peas inside the pod. Glue the ends of the pod together and trim the top with a calyx as before.*

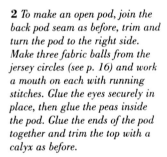

TINY PUMPKINS

You Will Need:
Burnt orange jersey fabric
Brown felt
3 mm (¹/8 in) black plastic beads
for eyes
Toy stuffing
Matching sewing and
buttonhole threads
Magnetic discs or brooch pins
Hot glue gun

Cutting Out:
Cut a rectangle, or square, of jersey measuring between 8–10 cm (3–4 in) wide and 6–8 cm (2³/8–3 in) long. Also cut a 1 cm (³/8 in) square of felt for the stalk.

1 *Make a tiny pumpkin, following the instructions given for the larger versions (p. 90). Fold the felt square in half and sew close to the side edge. Glue the stalk to the top of the pumpkin, then glue a magnet or brooch pin to the back of the pumpkin.*

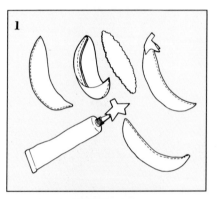

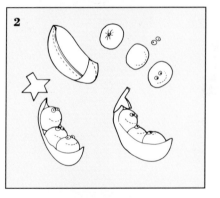

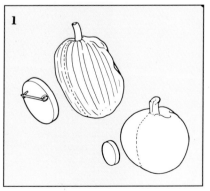

THE BASIC PUPPET

You Will Need:

Oddments of tracksuit jersey
fabric and acrylic jersey fleece
50 g (2 oz) of toy stuffing
Red, blue and yellow Velcro dots
Red cotton perlé
embroidery thread
Large buttons and embroidery
cotton, or a scrap of printed
cotton fabric
Matching sewing threads

Cutting Out:

*Trace off the same-size patterns on
pp. 100–101. Cut out the body
pieces from tracksuit jersey, using
the fleece side as the right side,
and the remaining pieces from
jersey fleece.*

*Take 6 mm (¹/₄ in) seam turnings
throughout.*

1 *Sew the hand pieces to the body
pieces, matching points A and B,
then press the seam turnings
towards the centre of the body.*

2 *Using matching sewing thread
for each colour of fabric, sew the
body pieces together, leaving the
base edges open. Turn under a
1 cm (³/₈ in) hem round the base
and handsew in place, working a
herringbone stitch over the raw
edge of the fabric.*

3 *Sew the ear pieces together in
pairs, leaving the straight edges
open. Trim the seam (see p. 19),
then turn each ear to the right
side. Now sew to the right side of
both sides of one head piece,
matching points C and D.*

4 *Sew the top and base dart on
both head pieces, snip the corners
then sew the head pieces together
with right sides facing, matching
top darts and points C and D and
leaving base edges open.*

MASTERS OF DISGUISE

*The eyes, noses, hair and hats
on these puppets are all
detachable, giving you the
opportunity to invent a host of
unique characters. You can
even alter the actor's mood
from winsome to villainous
simply by slanting the same
pair of eyes at different
angles. Here's your chance
to try your hand at
making faces!*

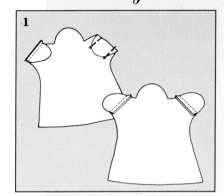

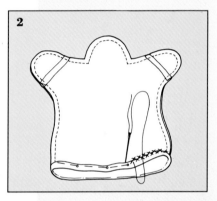

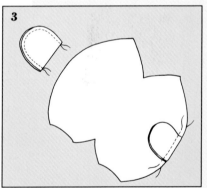

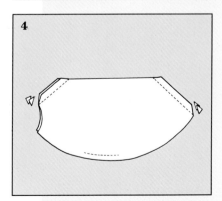

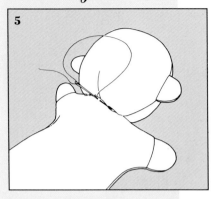

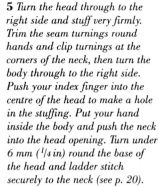

5 *Turn the head through to the right side and stuff very firmly. Trim the seam turnings round hands and clip turnings at the corners of the neck, then turn the body through to the right side. Push your index finger into the centre of the head to make a hole in the stuffing. Put your hand inside the body and push the neck into the head opening. Turn under 6 mm (¹/4 in) round the base of the head and ladder stitch securely to the neck (see p. 20).*

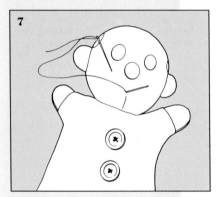

6 *Using the 'hooked' halves of the Velcro dots, handsew one red and two blue dots on the face in the nose and eye positions and a yellow dot directly above each ear to hold the hair or hat.*

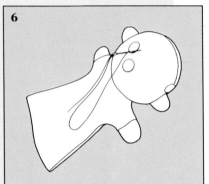

7 *Embroider the mouth with two straight stitches of cotton perlé, using a long needle and fastening off the ends of the thread inside the neck of the puppet. Sew two buttons down the centre front using a contrasting coloured embroidery cotton.*

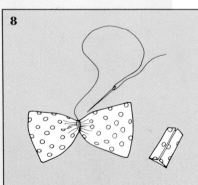

8 *As an alternative to buttons, make a bow tie from two squares of printed cotton, one 10 cm (4 in) and the other 3 cm (1¹/4 in). Fold the large square in half and sew all round the edge, leaving a 2.5 cm (1 in) opening in the centre of the long side. Turn to the right side through the opening and slipstitch gap closed. Press the side edges of the small square in to meet down the middle. Gather down the centre of the large square, draw up tightly and bind thread around the centre. Secure with a few stitches. Bind with the folded strip, sewing it in place. Sew the bow tie to the neck of the puppet.*

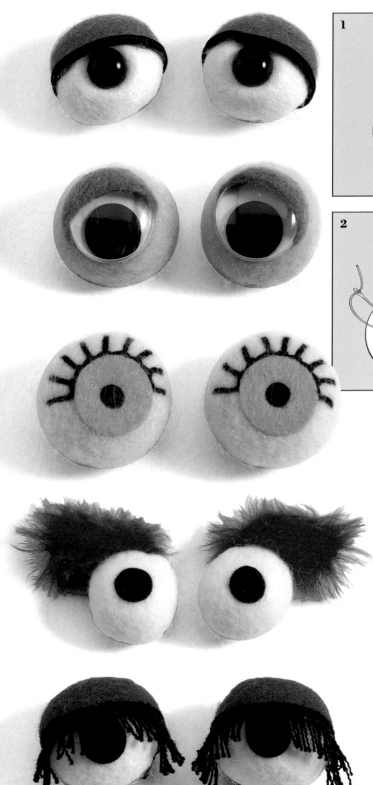

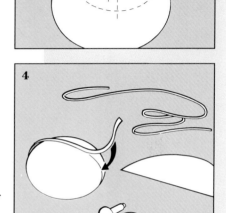

1

2 *Make a pair of fleece eyeballs and glue a 15 mm ($^5/8$ in) diameter circle of sealed turquoise felt (see p. 17) in the centre of each. Glue 6 mm ($^1/4$ in) diameter dots of black sealed felt in the centre for pupils, and work eyelashes in blanket stitch, using black cotton perlé.*

3 *Glue a 2 cm ($^3/4$ in) diameter circle of sealed turquoise felt off-centre on each of a pair of white felt eyeballs, then glue 1 cm ($^3/8$ in) diameter dots of sealed black felt in place for the pupils.*

4 *Make a pair of white felt eyeballs, fixing a 1 cm ($^3/8$ in) black toy eye in the centre of each circle before making up. Cut a 5 cm (2 in) diameter circle of lavender felt in half and glue to eyes to form eyelids, gluing excess to back of eye, then glue a piece of black Russia braid along the edge of each eyelid.*

3

4

2

5

EYES

You Will Need:
Scraps of felt, acrylic fleece, fur
fabric and black cotton canvas
Black safety toy eyes and glue-on
joggle eyes
Black Russia braid
Black cotton perlé
embroidery thread
Toy stuffing
Clear adhesive
Matching sewing threads

All the eyes are based on 5 cm (2 in) diameter stuffed fabric balls (see p. 16) with a blue 'looped' Velcro dot sewn on the back as the final step.

1 *Cut a 4 cm ($1^1/2$ in) diameter circle of lilac felt in half and glue each piece to a 2 cm ($^3/4$ in) joggle eye to form eyelids, gluing the excess fabric to the back of the eyes. Glue the eyes to a pair of blue fleece eyeballs.*

5 *Glue 1 cm ($^3/8$ in) diameter dots of sealed black felt to the centre of a pair of white felt eyeballs, then cut and glue on purple felt eyelids as in step 4. Make eyelashes by cutting a 1 x 10 cm ($^3/8$ x 4 in) strip of black canvas, having one long side running along the selvedge. Withdraw the long threads to fray the fabric, stopping 3 mm ($^1/8$ in) from the selvedge. Cut the canvas fringe in half and glue along the edge of each eyelid.*

6 *Glue 1 cm ($^3/8$ in) diameter dots of sealed black felt to the centre of a pair of white felt eyeballs. Cut two 2 x 3 cm ($^3/4$ x $1^3/4$ in) pieces of fur fabric for the eyebrows. Fold each piece in half with the wrong sides together. Oversew the longer sides together, then across both ends. Sew to the eyes, slanting the fur in opposite directions to make a pair.*

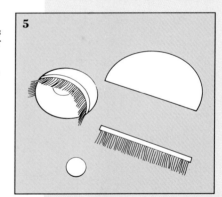

6

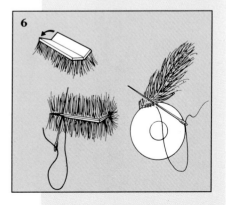

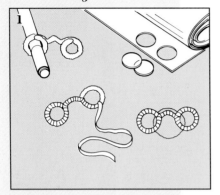

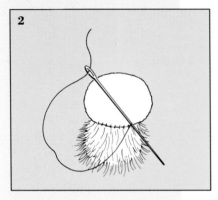

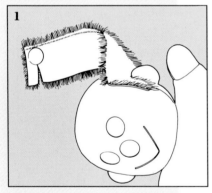

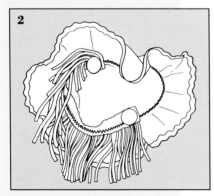

NOSES

1 *Make a round ball nose in white stretch towelling. Shape glasses from a pipe-cleaner, winding it round the barrel of a marker pen. Bind the pipe-cleaner tightly with narrow gold ribbon, then glue circles of clear plastic behind each opening. Glue securely in place on the nose.*

2 *Make an oval nose from white stretch towelling, and cut a 2 cm (³/4 in) square of fur fabric for the moustache. Fold in half, wrong sides together, and oversew all round, then position and oversew to the base of the nose.*

You Will Need:
Scraps of felt, acrylic fleece,
jersey, fur fabric and
stretch towelling
A pipe-cleaner, narrow gold
ribbon, and a scrap of
clear plastic film
Toy stuffing
Clear adhesive
Matching sewing threads

All the noses are based on 5 cm (2 in) or 7 cm (2³/4 in) diameter stuffed fabric balls (see p. 16) with a red 'looped' Velcro dot sewn on the back as the final step.

Using either measurement, make balls of felt or fleece for round noses and jersey or stretch towelling for oval versions.

HAIR AND HATS

1 Bald head: *Cut a 5 x 18 cm (2 x 7 in) piece of fur fabric, having the fur pile running parallel to the shorter sides, and a matching piece of felt. Sew the pieces together along the top edge, then glue both wrong sides together. When set, cut a 2 cm (³/4 in) long slit up from the base edge, 1 cm (³/8 in) in from each end to fit over the ears.*

2 Mob-cap: *Cut a 28 cm (11 in) diameter circle of printed cotton and seal edge with fabric sealer. Turn under 6 mm (¹/4 in) all round, then sew along the centre of a length of ricrac braid using a machine stitch close to the folded brim edge. Work a gathering thread around the circle 4 cm (1¹/2 in) in from the edge, draw up to fit round the head and fasten off the ends. Even out the gathers and cut a 20 cm (8 in) length of upholstery fringing. Using a narrow zigzag stitch and working over the gathering line, sew the hat to the fringe heading, then zigzag stitch over the remainder of the gathering line twice to secure the gathers.*

You Will Need:
Oddments of felt, fur fabric,
printed cotton fabric and
cotton jersey
Ribbon, ricrac braid, gold cord
and a feather
Upholstery and
lampshade fringing
Chunky and double knitting yarns
Stiff card
Clear adhesive and anti-fray
fabric sealer
Matching sewing threads

After making up, place hair or hat on puppet, position yellow 'looped' Velcro dots to correspond with those on the head, and sew securely in place.

Take 6 mm (¹/4 in) seam turnings throughout

▶ *Mix and match hats, noses and eyes to create a whole theatre of characters, from a traditional boater-hatted schoolboy to an exotic magician from the Orient.*

3 Pillbox: *From felt, cut a 13 x 31 cm (5 x 12¼ in) rectangle and an 11 cm (4½ in) diameter circle. Join the short sides of the rectangle and trim the seam. Sew the top edge of the hat to the circle with right sides together, then trim the seam. Turn the hat to the right side and glue a 20 cm (8 in) double layer of lampshade fringing to the back inside base edge of the hat. Sew a feather on the front of the hat and trim with a coil of gold cord, glued at the base of the feather.*

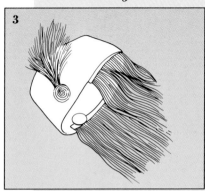

4 Bobble hat: *Cut a 30 cm (12 in) square of cotton jersey. Join the two sides parallel to the selvedge and press the seam open. Turn under a 5 cm (2 in) hem at one end and work a zigzag stitch over the cut edge. Gather the remaining end of the hat, draw up thread tightly and fasten off. Turn hat to right side. Make a bobble from double knitting yarn wound round two discs of card placed together, both with a hole cut in the middle. Cut the yarn at the outer edge and tie a length of yarn around the bobble between the two card discs. Remove the card and sew the bobble to the top of the hat.*

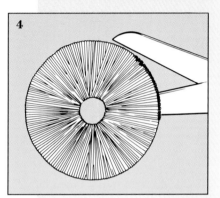

5 *Fold up a 3 cm (1¼ in) brim round the hemmed end. Wind chunky yarn round your index finger five times and sew together to make a bunch of loops. Position and sew loops securely to the inside front edge of the brim.*

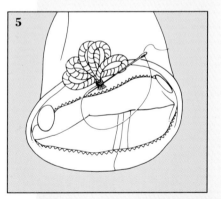

6 Headscarf: *Cut a 30 cm (12 in) square of printed cotton. Turn under and sew down a tiny hem all round, then fold in half diagonally and pull tightly to stretch the fabric along this fold. Place the scarf on the puppet and tie tightly under the chin with a double knot, securing the knot with a few stitches. Make a bunch of yarn loops as for the bobble hat and sew in place inside the top edge of the scarf. There is no need to sew Velcro dots to this scarf.*

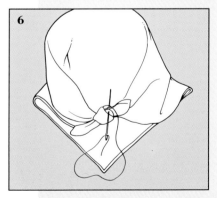

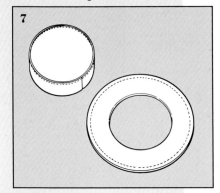

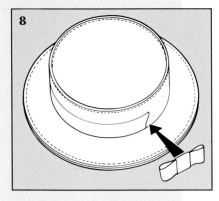

7 Boater: *From felt, cut two 15 cm (6 in) diameter circles for the brim, then cut a 9 cm (3¹/₂ in) diameter circular opening from the centre of each. Also cut an 11 cm (4¹/₂ in) diameter circle for the crown, and a 5 x 31 cm (2 x 12¹/₄ in) rectangle for the side piece. With the two brim pieces together, sew all round, close to outer edge. Sew the short sides of the side piece and trim the seam, then turn to right side. Sew one edge of this band to the crown piece, then trim the seam.*

8 *Sew the side and crown piece to the opening in the brim, then trim the seam. Position and sew on Velcro dots, then glue the ribbon band round the side, covering the join with a ribbon bow. Cut a 10 cm (4 in) diameter circle of card and glue inside the crown to make a flat top.*

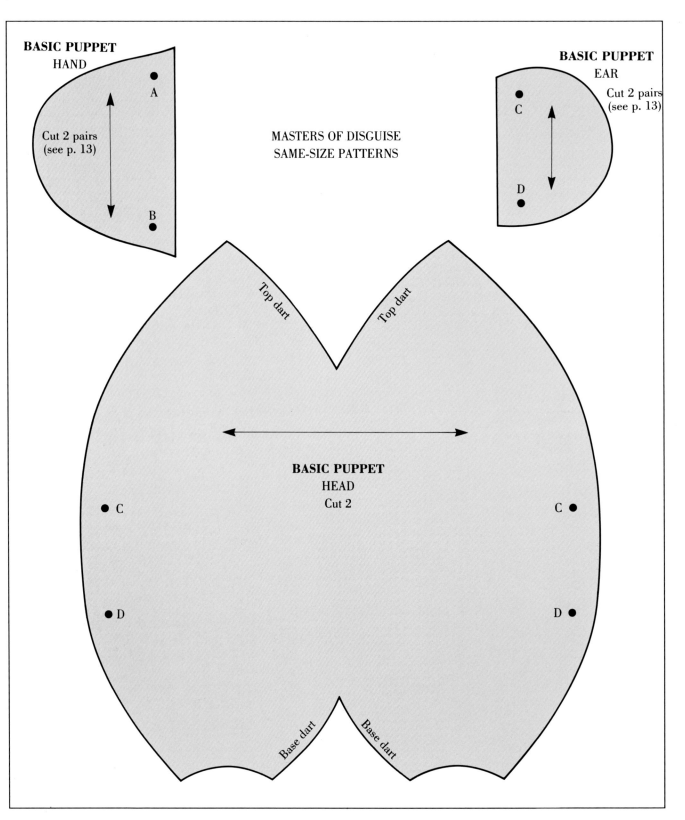

BASIC PUPPET
HAND

A

Cut 2 pairs
(see p. 13)

B

MASTERS OF DISGUISE
SAME-SIZE PATTERNS

BASIC PUPPET
EAR

Cut 2 pairs
(see p. 13)

C

D

Top dart   Top dart

C   C

BASIC PUPPET
HEAD
Cut 2

D   D

Base dart   Base dart

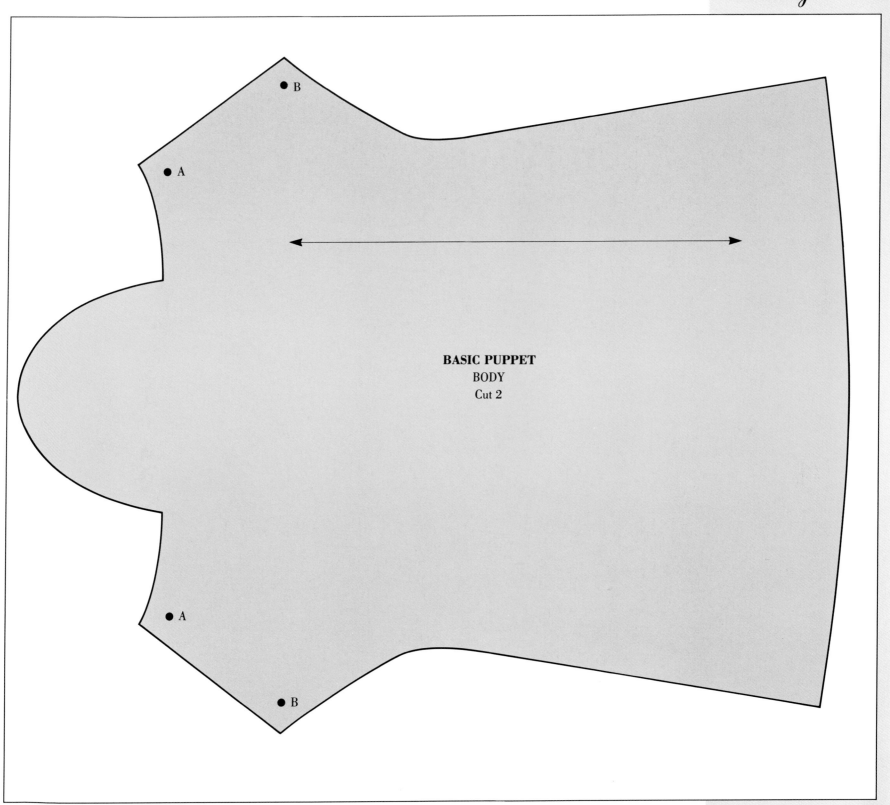

B

A

BASIC PUPPET
BODY
Cut 2

A

B

RAINBOW ARK

You Will Need:

40 cm (¹/₂ yd) of 115 cm (45 in)
wide rainbow-striped
cotton fabric
20 cm (¹/₄ yd) of 115 cm (45 in)
wide yellow cotton poplin
10 cm (¹/₈ yd) of 115 cm wide
red multi-coloured spotted
cotton fabric
60 cm (²/₃ yd) of 115 cm (45 in)
wide cream cotton poplin
50 cm (⁵/₈ yd) of 150 cm (60 in)
wide medium-weight
Terylene wadding
Scraps of white, blue and green
cotton poplin
Small amounts of iron-on bonding
web and extra fine
iron-on interfacing
1.60 m (1³/₄ yd) of 2.5 cm (1 in)
wide red bias binding and
2.20 m (2¹/₂ yd) of 2.5 cm (1 in)
wide blue bias binding
A 25 cm (10 in) red nylon zip
Red, yellow, green, black and
white relief outline fabric paints
A small amount of toy stuffing
Hot glue gun
Matching sewing threads

Cutting Out:

*Draw out the measurements-only
pattern pieces on pp. 108–109 on
to plain paper and cut out.
Cutting a matching wadding and
cream poplin lining piece to
accompany each piece, cut out the
ark pieces from the fabrics stated
on the patterns. Fuse the bonding
web to the blue and green poplin.
Cut out four windows from the
bonded blue poplin and a door
from the bonded green poplin.
Trace off the same-size dove
pattern and draw round the
outline with a pencil on to the
wrong side of a piece of interfaced
white poplin, roughly twice the
size of the dove pattern.*

*Take 6 mm (¹/₄ in) seam turnings
throughout*

1 *Remove the backing paper from
the bonding web, then position
and fuse the door and windows on
to the cabin front and back pieces.
Using the fabric paints, outline
each piece to seal the cut edges,
then draw the door planks,
doorknob and window bars and
leave until completely set.*

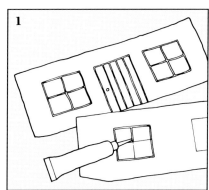

2 *Placing a layer of wadding in
between, tack each matching top
piece and lining piece together
round the outside edge. Bind one
long side of each roof piece with
red bias binding by sewing the
binding right sides together with
the top fabric. Fold the binding
over the edge to the lining side
and sew down by hand, following
the machine stitching line.*

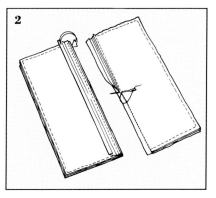

3 *Insert the zip between the two
bound edges of the roof. When
stitching each of the following
seams, start sewing 6 mm (¹/₄ in)
in from one end, and finish 6 mm
(¹/₄ in) in from the other end. With
the lining sides together, sew the
remaining long side of each roof
piece to the top edge of the cabin
front and back pieces. The seam
turnings will show on the right
side of the work. With the right
sides together, sew the deck
triangles to the cabin side pieces,
then neaten each seam by working
a zigzag stitch over the raw edges.*

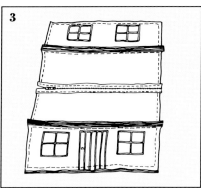

◀ *Even beginners will find these
charming rainbow animals simple
to sew. The ark makes a tidy home
to keep them in as well as a
colourful accessory for the nursery.*

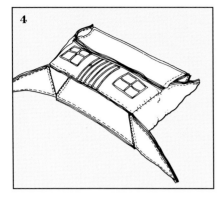

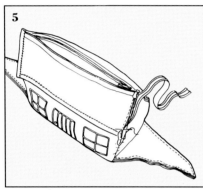

4 With the right sides together, join the side edges of the cabin front and back pieces to the bottom portion of the cabin side pieces, then neaten the seams with a zigzag stitch as before. Turn the cabin through to the right side.

5 With the lining sides together so that the seam turnings will show on the right side, sew the side edges of the roof to the top portion of the cabin side pieces. With red binding, bind the long base edges of the roof, then bind the four side edges. Sew the ends of the side binding together by hand at the apex of the roof.

MULTI-COLOURED
ANIMALS SAME-SIZE
PATTERNS

PILLOW PETS
CHARTED PATTERNS:
1 sq = 5 cm (2 in)

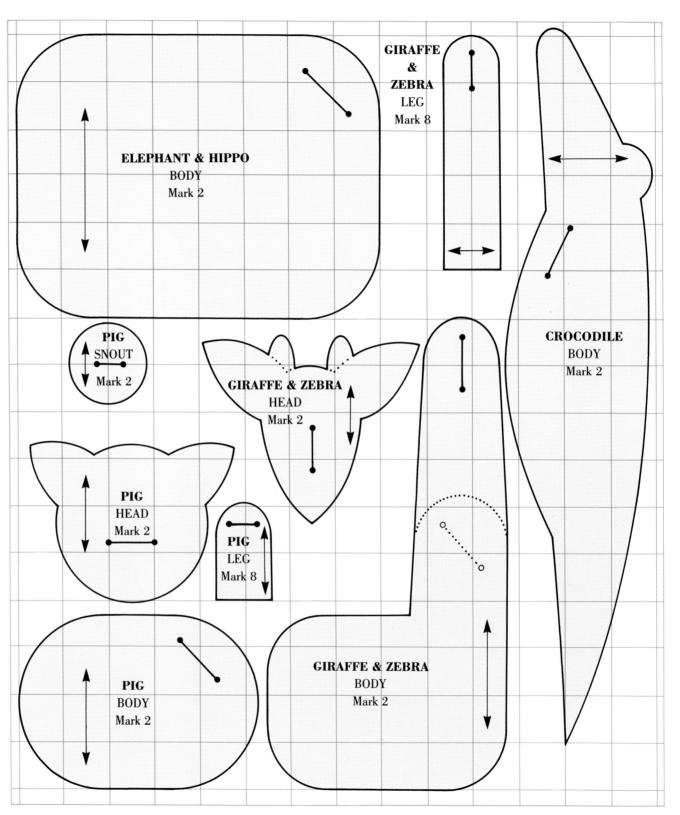

ELEPHANT & HIPPO
BODY
Mark 2

GIRAFFE
&
ZEBRA
LEG
Mark 8

CROCODILE
BODY
Mark 2

PIG
SNOUT
Mark 2

GIRAFFE & ZEBRA
HEAD
Mark 2

PIG
HEAD
Mark 2

PIG
LEG
Mark 8

GIRAFFE & ZEBRA
BODY
Mark 2

PIG
BODY
Mark 2

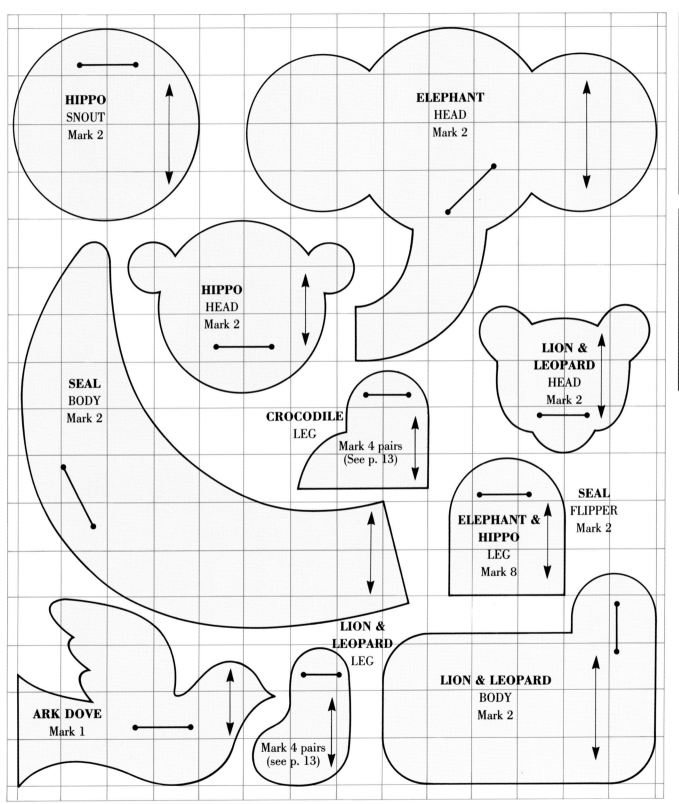

HIPPO
SNOUT
Mark 2

ELEPHANT
HEAD
Mark 2

HIPPO
HEAD
Mark 2

SEAL
BODY
Mark 2

CROCODILE
LEG
Mark 4 pairs
(See p. 13)

**LION &
LEOPARD**
HEAD
Mark 2

**ELEPHANT &
HIPPO**
LEG
Mark 8

SEAL
FLIPPER
Mark 2

**LION &
LEOPARD**
LEG
Mark 4 pairs
(see p. 13)

LION & LEOPARD
BODY
Mark 2

ARK DOVE
Mark 1

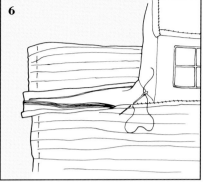

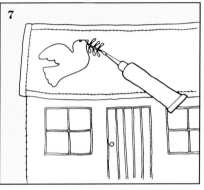

6 *With the lining sides together as before, sew the side edges of the deck triangles and the base edge of the cabin to the top edge of each hull piece. Bind each seam, using blue binding.*

7 *With lining sides together, sew all round the curved base seam of the hull, sewing right up to each end of the seam, then bind with blue binding. Remove all the tacking threads. Using the directions given for the animals which follow, make up the dove and glue to the roof with the glue gun. Decorate the dove with fabric paints and paint an olive branch on the roof, then leave to set.*

Rainbow Ark & Animals

MULTI-COLOURED ANIMALS

You Will Need
For All 18 Animals:

Approx. 15 cm (6 in) of
90 cm (36 in) wide cotton
printed and plain fabrics in
each of nine colours
1.30 m (1½ yd) of
90 cm (36 in) wide extra fine
iron-on interfacing
15 cm (6 in) of yellow
ricrac braid
1 m (1⅛ yd) of white double
knitting yarn
225 g (8 oz) of toy stuffing
Red, yellow, blue, green, pink,
black and white relief outline
fabric paints
Sharp embroidery scissors
Pair of blunt-ended tweezers
Hot glue gun
Matching sewing threads

Cutting Out:

*Trace off the same-size pattern
pieces on pp. 104–105. Draw
round the dotted lines when
cutting out the zebra body and
head patterns. Collect all the
pieces for one animal together
and, on the wrong side of the
interfacing, draw round the
pattern pieces with pencil,
marking out the number of pieces
directed on the patterns (this
number will make a pair of
animals) and leaving at least
1 cm (³/₈ in) between each piece.
Cut roughly round the outside of
this marked piece and cut another
piece of interfacing the same
shape. Fuse each piece of
interfacing to the wrong side of
the chosen fabric, then repeat for
all the remaining animals. For
each pair of lions and leopards
you will also need to cut a 15 x
3 cm (6 x 1¼ in) strip of fabric
for the tails.*

1 *Pin the matching marked and plain interfaced pieces right sides together, then sew all round each marked outline, using a small machine stitch. Cut out each animal piece, cutting 3 mm ($^1/8$ in) outside the sewing line, then clip and notch turnings round the curved sections (see p.18). Carefully cut the marked opening in the top layer of fabric only using a pair of sharp embroidery scissors. Turn each animal piece to the right side through this opening, using the tweezers to push out the corners.*

2 *Stuff each piece lightly, using the tweezers to push the stuffing in place. Close each opening by oversewing the cut edge. Hot glue the pieces together, spreading adhesive over the stitched openings and holding the pieces in place until the glue sets.*

3 *Make up all the animals in the same manner. Make the lion and leopard tails by joining the long sides of the tail strip, with right sides together and taking a 6 mm ($^1/4$ in) seam turning. Turn the tail through to the right side, then cut into two 6 cm ($2^3/8$ in) lengths. Cut the yarn into eight equal lengths, thread through a thick, blunt-ended needle, then thread the needle and yarn through both tail pieces to stuff. Trim away the excess yarn, push in raw edges of each tail and seal with a dab of glue, then glue it to the back seam of the animal. Glue a ricrac 'ruff' round the lion's head before gluing it in place on the body.*

4 *Following the photographs, decorate the animals with the fabric paints, leaving the front side to set completely before turning over and decorating the back. To avoid making any mistakes, you may prefer to draw the features on to the animal first with an air-vanishing embroiderer's pen before painting. The pen's marks will disappear within 24 hours.*

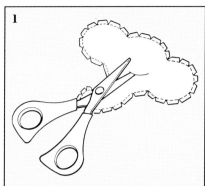

1

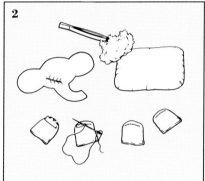

2

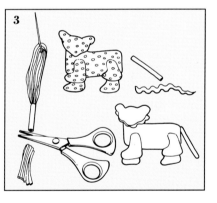

3

4

Rainbow Ark & Animals

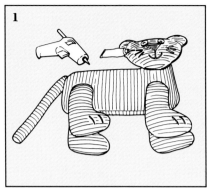

PILLOW PETS

You Will Need
For Each Animal:
40 cm ($\frac{1}{2}$ yd) of 90 cm (36 in) wide plain or printed cotton fabric
40 cm ($\frac{1}{2}$ yd) of 90 cm (36 in) wide extra fine iron-on interfacing
350 g (12 oz) of toy stuffing
Two 2 cm ($\frac{3}{4}$ in) diameter buttons
Black embroidery thread
45 cm ($\frac{1}{2}$ yd) of jumbo ricrac braid for the lion's ruff
Relief outline fabric paints
Hot glue gun
Matching sewing threads

Cutting Out:
Enlarge the hippo and lion pattern pieces on pp. 104–105 to 400% (either by photocopier or by charting on to graph paper – see p. 12) and follow the cutting out instructions given for the multi-coloured animals (p. 106). To alter the direction of an animal's face, reverse the pattern pieces when marking out. For each lion or leopard tail you will also need to cut a 25 x 10 cm (10 x 4 in) strip of fabric.

▶ *Make pillow pets from any of the multi-coloured animal patterns, choosing fabrics that are bold, colourful and fun.*

1 *Make up the pillow pets as directed for the multi-coloured animals (pp. 106–107). Join the long sides of the lion or leopard tail strip, taking a 6 mm ($\frac{1}{4}$ in) turning. Gather round one end, draw up tightly and fasten off. Turn the strip through to the right side, stuff lightly, then gather the remaining end as before, pushing the raw edges inwards. Glue the tail to the back seam of the animal, then sew the top of the tail to the body. Position and sew the button eyes in place with embroidery thread, then decorate the animals with fabric paints as before and leave to set completely.*

5 cm (2 in)

ARK
CABIN SIDE
Cut 2 from yellow poplin

8.5 cm (3 $\frac{1}{4}$ in)

10 cm (4 in)

10 cm (4 in)

ARK
DECK
Cut 2 from yellow poplin

11 cm (4 $\frac{1}{2}$ in)

5.5 cm (2 $\frac{1}{4}$ in)

17 cm (6 $\frac{3}{4}$ in)

5 cm (2 in)

ARK
WINDOW

5 cm (2 in)

5 cm (2 in)

ARK
DOOR

7.5 cm (3 in)

10 cm (4 in)

ARK
CABIN FRONT
CABIN BACK
ROOF
Cut 2 from yellow poplin and 2 from red spotted cotton

25 cm (10 in)

27.5 cm (10 $\frac{3}{4}$ in)

32.5 cm (12 $\frac{3}{4}$ in)

Place on fold (see p. 12)

ARK
HULL
Cut 2 from rainbow-striped cotton

27.5 cm (10 $\frac{3}{4}$ in)

RAINBOW ARK
MEASUREMENTS-ONLY PATTERNS